HOW WE GOT THE BIBLE

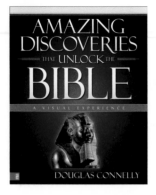

Amazing Discoveries That Unlock the Bible
Douglas Connelly
ISBN-13: 978-0-310-25799-8
ISBN-10: 0-310-25799-9

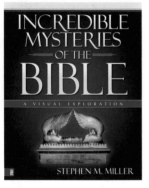

Incredible Mysteries of the Bible
Stephen M. Miller
ISBN-13: 978-0-310-25594-9
ISBN-10: 0-310-25594-5

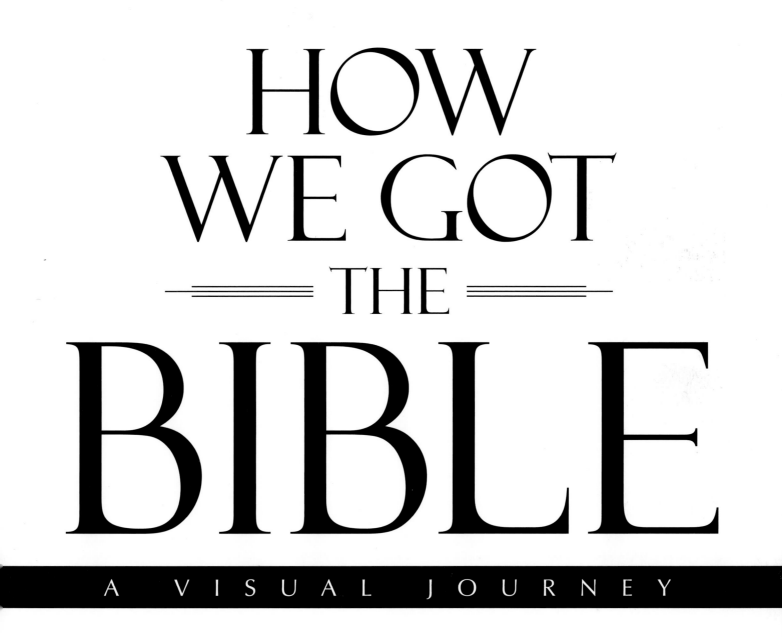

HOW WE GOT THE BIBLE

A VISUAL JOURNEY

CLINTON E. ARNOLD

ZONDERVAN®

ZONDERVAN.com/
AUTHORTRACKER
follow your favorite authors

How We Got the Bible
Copyright © 2008 by Clinton E. Arnold

Requests for information should be addressed to:

Zondervan, *Grand Rapids, Michigan 49530*

Library of Congress Cataloging-in-Publication Data

Arnold, Clinton E.
    How we got the Bible : a visual journey / Clinton E. Arnold.
       p. cm. — (Zondervan visual reference series)
    ISBN-13: 978-0-310-25306-8
    ISBN-10: 0-310-25306-3
    1. Bible—History. I. Title.
BS445.A76 2007
220.09—dc22

2007000427

Interior design by Ron Huizenga

Printed in Hong Kong

08 09 10 11 12 • 10 9 8 7 6 5 4 3 2 1

TABLE OF CONTENTS

THE OLDEST FORMS OF THE BIBLE EVER DISCOVERED

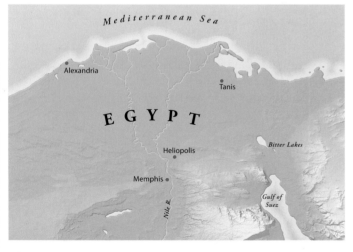

The text of the Bible that we use today is well-attested to by many ancient copies. Although none of the original documents survive (such as the actual hand-written form of the first five books of the Bible written by Moses 3,400 years ago) we do have some very old copies of portions of the Bible. Some of these are actually very close in date to the originals. The oldest form of the Bible that has ever been discovered is over 2,600 years old. It is a portion of the book of Numbers that was written on silver leaves and discovered in 1979 near Jerusalem. The oldest portion of the New Testament that has been discovered is a papyrus fragment of John's gospel found in the sands of Egypt. It was copied roughly thirty years after John wrote the original draft of his gospel. Discoveries of ancient texts continue to be made. Caves near the Dead Sea in Israel, storerooms in monasteries, and excavations in Egypt have all turned up manuscripts in recent years. Perhaps one of the most surprising places scholars have found Bible manuscripts in recent years has been in libraries and museums. Some of these museums contain boxes of unclassified pieces of ancient manuscripts that require enormous time and expertise to sort through and identify.

◄ **ONE OF THE DEAD SEA SCROLLS** The caves at Qumran yielded the oldest manuscripts of the Old Testament ever to be discovered. This is a scroll of the Psalms that measures thirteen feet when unrolled. It contains forty-one Psalms from the last third of the book. It was written in Hebrew and dates from about AD 30–50. It is known as "Elizabeth Bechtel Psalms Scroll" after the American philanthropist and is designated 11QPsᵃ. It was discovered in 1956.

◄ **THE OLDEST FRAGMENT OF THE NEW TESTAMENT** This is a portion of John's gospel (18:31–33, 37–38) that dates to about AD 125. It is often referred to as the "Rylands Fragment" since it is housed in the John Rylands Library in Manchester, England. It was discovered in Egypt in the 1920s.

◄ **THE OLDEST FRAGMENT OF THE HEBREW BIBLE UNTIL THE DISCOVERY OF THE DEAD SEA SCROLLS IN 1947** This text is known as the "Nash Papyrus" and dates to the first or second century BC. It was discovered in Egypt in 1902. The scroll contains the Ten Commandments and the *shema* (Exodus 20:1–17 and Deuteronomy 6:4–9). It was purchased in 1902 by W. L. Nash from an Egyptian Antique dealer.

THE OLDEST MANUSCRIPT OF THE PROPHETS UNTIL THE DISCOVERIES AT QUMRAN

This is a leaf from Codex Cairensis (C) that dates to AD 895. It was copied by the famous scribe, Moses ben Asher, at Tiberias, near the Sea of Galilee. This leaf is the text of Zechariah 14 and the beginning of Malachi.

◄ **THE OLDEST FORM OF ANY PORTION OF THE HEBREW BIBLE** The two thin silver rolls contain the priestly blessing from Numbers 6:24–26. They date to the seventh century BC, the time of the prophet Jeremiah. They were discovered in an excavation of a burial tomb near Jerusalem in 1979.

ALPHABETS, ANIMAL HIDES, AND PAPYRUS

It is almost difficult for us to imagine a world without paper, pencils, pens, and now, word processors. In the ancient world, writing was a much more expensive and time-consuming endeavor. Few individuals would have owned a copy of the Bible because of the enormous cost of purchasing a hand-copied manuscript. Bibles were owned by communities—synagogues and churches. The earliest forms of writing were wedge-like characters engraved on stone. No biblical texts were written in this Cuneiform script. Most of the ancient copies of the Bible were written on papyrus or vellum. Papyrus was a reed that grew in the Nile river of Egypt that could be dried and fashioned into a type of paper. Vellum was a specially prepared skin from an animal, such as a cow or a goat. This was a durable material and was sometimes erased and reused.

▶ **THE PAPYRUS IS HARVESTED, FLATTENED, DRIED, AND CUT INTO STRIPS**
It is then laid on a flat surface and placed in a criss-cross fashion to form the paper.

◀ **AN ANCIENT STYLUS AND INKWELL USED IN WRITING ON PAPYRUS**
These materials were used by a scribe who lived during the 22nd dynasty (945–712 BC). The papyrus text is a portion of the Egyptian Book of the Dead.

בביתו ומדבר כלשון עמו אחר הדברים האלה אמר המלך לחכמים ידעי העתים כי כן דבר
כשר חמת המלך אחשורוש זכר את ושתי ואת אשר עשתה ישרי דת ודין והקרב אליו כרשנא שתר
ואת אשר נגזר עליה ויאמרו נערי המלך משרתיו יבקשו למלך ישיש מרס מרסנא ממוכן שבעת שרי פרס ומדי
נערות בתולות טובות מראה ויפקד המלך פקידים בכל מדינות הישבים ראשנה במלכות כדת מה לעשות
מלכותו ויקבצו את כל נערה בתולה טובת מראה אל על אשר לא עשתה את מאמר המלך
שושן הבירה אל בית הנשים אל יד הגא סרים המלך שמר הנשים ויאמר מומכן לפני המלך
ונתון תמרקיהן והנערה אשר תיטב בעיני המלך תמלך תחת והשרים לא על המלך לבדו עותה ושתי המלכה כי על כל
ושתי וייטב הדבר בעיני המלך ויעש כן איש יהודי השרים ועל כל העמים אשר בכל מדינות המלך אחשורוש
היה בשושן הבירה ושמו מרדכי בן יאיר בן שמעי בן קיש כי יצא דבר המלכה על כל הנשים להבזות בעליהן בעיניהן
איש ימיני אשר הגלה מירושלם עם הגלה אשר הגלתה באמרם המלך אחשורוש אמר להביא את ושתי המלכה
עם יכניה מלך יהודה אשר הגלה נבוכדנצר מלך בבל ויהי לפניו ולא באה והיום הזה תאמרנה שרות פרס ומדי אשר
אמן את הדסה היא אסתר בת דדו כי אין לה אב ואם והנערה שמעו את דבר המלכה לכל שרי המלך וכדי בזיון וקצף
יפת תאר וטובת מראה ובמות אביה ואמה לקחה מרדכי לו אם טוב על המלך יצא דבר מלכות מלפניו ויכתב בדתי
לבת ויהי כהשמע דבר המלך ודתו ובהקבץ נערות רבות פרס ומדי ולא יעבור אשר לא תבוא ושתי לפני המלך
אל שושן הבירה ותלקח אסתר אל בית המלך אחשורוש ומלכותה יתן המלך לרעותה הטובה ממנה
אל יד הגי שמר הנשים ותיטב הנערה בעיניו ותשא חסד ונשמע פתגם המלך אשר יעשה בכל מלכותו כי רבה
לפניו ויבהל את תמרוקיה ואת מנותה לתת לה ואת שבע היא וכל הנשים יתנו יקר לבעליהן למגדול ועד קטן
הנערות הראית לתת לה מבית המלך וישנה ואת נערותיה וייטב הדבר בעיני המלך והשרים ויעש המלך כדבר
לטוב בית הנשים לא הגידה אסתר את עמה ואת מולדתה ממוכן וישלח ספרים אל כל מדינות המלך אל מדינה
כי מרדכי צוה עליה אשר לא תגיד ובכל יום ויום מר דכי ומדינה ככתבה ואל עם ועם כלשונו להיות כל איש שרר

▼ Papyrus reeds growing along the bank of the Nile River in Egypt.

THE EPIC OF GILGAMESH

Written on twelve clay tablets in Cuneiform script in the Akkadian language, these documents date to the seventh century BC. They were found at Nineveh (in modern Iraq, near Mosul) at the site of a library belonging to an Assyrian king named Ashurbanipal (668–627 BC). They relate the exploits of a king, Gilgamesh, who ruled in the area in the third millennium BC (around 2700–2500 BC), prior to the time of Abraham.

► **VELLUM WAS A POPULAR WRITING MATERIAL FOR BIBLICAL MANUSCRIPTS** Here the animal hide is being stretched and prepared for its use in a manuscript.

◄ **A SCROLL OF THE HEBREW BIBLE** This is a nineteenth-century parchment scroll of the third division of the Old Testament.

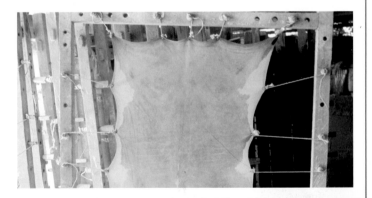

◄ **A FINISHED PIECE OF PAPYRUS READY FOR WRITING** The material could be prepared in a manner that would be conducive to the creation of a scroll or with leaves to be bound in a book form (a codex).

► **A LEAF FROM CODEX LENINGRADENSIS** This is the end of Genesis and the beginning of Exodus.

THE PRINCIPAL MANUSCRIPT
BEHIND THE OLD TESTAMENT

▲ **THE TEXT OF GENESIS 1 IN THE HEBREW BIBLE MOST SCHOLARS USE TODAY** It is published by the United Bible Societies. Although the editors of this text consulted many manuscripts and versions, Codex Leningradensis served as the primary basis.

Virtually every Bible read today is deeply indebted to a very important manuscript of the Hebrew Bible that is 1,000 years old. It is called Codex Leningradensis, an early eleventh-century AD manuscript that is housed in the Russian Public Library in Leningrad. It is the oldest dated manuscript of the complete Hebrew Bible. A beautiful volume of 491 folios, or leaves, with three columns per page, it was completed in AD 1010 in Cairo, Egypt. According to a scribal note in the volume, it was copied from exemplars produced by a famous Masoretic scholar named Aharon ben Asher who was part of a long line of scribes. The Masoretes (from the Hebrew word *masorah,* meaning "transmission of traditions") were Hebrew scholars devoted to a meticulous preservation of the Bible and its proper pronunciation. Codex Leningradensis (designated B 19ᵃ or "L") has long been regarded as being a faithful representation of the text of the Hebrew Bible. The accuracy of this assumption has been significantly bolstered by the exceptional degree of agreements between the Dead Sea Scroll texts of the Bible and the text of Codex Leningradensis.

▲ An illumination from Codex Leningradensis.

A LEAF FROM THE ALEPPO CODEX

This manuscript was copied in AD 935 and kept in the Aleppo Synagogue in Syria. Originally complete, one-quarter of it was destroyed when the Aleppo synagogue was set on fire in 1948. Now in Israel, this manuscript was given priority in the creation of the *Hebrew University Bible*.

▶ **A PORTION OF THE MASORAH IN CODEX LENINGRADENSIS** The marginal notations throughout the manuscript are called "Masoretic notes." This manuscript contains 60,000 scribal notes. They were largely concerned with detailed word statistics, with the overall goal of accurately preserving and transmitting the text.

▼ **A DRAWING OF THE CITY OF TIBERIAS ALONG THE SEA OF GALILEE FROM THE MID–1800s** Many generations of Masoretes (scribes) worked here, especially throughout the first millennium.

THE HEBREW BIBLE IS TRANSLATED INTO GREEK

After Alexander the Great followed his imperialistic notions and extended his kingdom far into the East, Greek became a world language. To succeed in business and commerce, people in Syria, Egypt, Israel, Asia Minor, North Africa, and Italy all needed to speak and write in Greek. During this period many Jews took up residence in all of these lands, but Egypt, in particular, became home to many thousands of Jews. As they lost facility in their native tongues (Hebrew and Aramaic), there was a growing desire and need for accessibilty to the Scriptures in the language with which they were now most at home—Greek. To facilitate this need, Jewish scholars in Egypt undertook the translation of the Hebrew Bible into Greek roughly two to three centuries before the time of Christ. According to a Jewish tradition that is largely discounted, the translation was actually commissioned and subsidized by an Egyptian ruler, Ptolemy II Philadelphus (285–247 BC). This story, told in the *Letter of Aristeas,* claims that seventy scribes worked on this translation. Thus, the product was called the *septuagint,* after the Greek word for "seventy." The text of the Septuagint is preserved in nearly 2,000 ancient Greek manuscripts.

▲ The first page of Genesis from the Septuagint published by the United Bible Societies.

▲ **A MAP OF EGYPT** Philo of Alexandria claims that as many as a million Jews lived in Egypt during his time (first century AD). The largest population of Jews was in the city of Alexandria.

◄ An illumination from a Greek version of the Old Testament published in 1565 known as the Ruskin Septuagint.

◄ A PORTION OF THE SEPTUAGINT FOUND AT QUMRAN These are a collection of fragments from the book of Leviticus found at Cave 4. It has been designated 4Q120papLXX Lev[b]. Courtesy Israel Antiquities Authority.

▲ THE EARLIEST SURVIVING PORTIONS OF THE GREEK BIBLE These fragments are of portions of the book of Deuteronomy (chs. 23–28) and date to the second century BC. Interestingly, the scroll of which they were a part had been used in the wrapping of a mummy. It is designated as Rylands Papyrus 458.

▼ A LEAF FROM CODEX SINAITICUS OF THE TEXT OF ISAIAH 52–53 This is one of the oldest Greek parchment manuscripts of the Old Testament.

THE SEPTUAGINT

The form of the Septuagint used by scholars and Bible teachers today. It was edited by Alfred Rahlfs and published by the United Bible Socieites. It takes into account all available manuscripts of the Septuagint.

THE HEBREW BIBLE INTO MANY OTHER LANGUAGES

The Bible held a cental role for the piety of the Jewish people. God told his people, "these commandments that I give you today are to be upon your hearts. Impress them on your children. Talk about them when you sit at home and when you walk along the road, when you lie down and when you get up" (Deut. 6:6–7). It is only natural that God's people would want the Scripture in the langauge that they used when they were at home and were walking along the road. After the exile (sixth century BC), Aramaic became the common language throughout the Persian empire, including the land of Israel. This was the first language into which the Hebrew Bible was translated. Known as the *targums*, these manuscripts represented not only an Aramaic translation of the Bible but contain interpretive comments as well. The early Christians also cherished the Old Testament. They were largely responsible for the translation of the Old Testament into languages such as Syriac, Coptic, and Latin.

◄ **ACCORDING TO GENESIS 11,** the tower of Babel incident resulted in the division of humanity into a wide variety of language groups. This is a 1563 depiction of the tower by the Flemish painter Pieter Bruegel the Elder.

▶ **A LATIN MANUSCRIPT OF EXODUS COPIED IN AD 1170** The text includes many notations.

▲ **FRAGMENTS OF AN ARAMAIC TARGUM FOUND AT QUMRAN** Courtesy Israel Antiquities Authority.

▶ **A PAGE FROM THE BOOK OF PSALMS** translated into Syriac dating from the seventh century AD.

▼ **A COPTIC (EGYPTIAN) MANUSCRIPT** of Jeremiah dated to the fourth century AD.

THE DEAD SEA SCROLLS

In 1947, a young Bedouin shepherd looking for a lost goat discovered a cave with a clay pot containing a very ancient scroll. This was the first of a huge cache of manusripts discovered in eleven caves in this area over the next twenty years. These "Dead Sea Scrolls" became the most significant archaeological find of the century. Among the twenty-eight nearly complete scrolls and the 100,000 fragments of another 875 manuscripts, multiple portions of every book of the Hebrew Bible (except Esther) were present. These Hebrew, Aramaic, and Greek manuscripts became the oldest representatives of the Old Testament text available, pushing back the date of our earliest biblical manuscripts by 1,000 years. They also demonstrate an extraordinary correspondence with the form of the Hebrew text that we already possessed. The finds also included documents reflecting the lives and beliefs of this Jewish separatist community settled on the northwest bank of the Dead Sea about twelve miles from Jerusalem. Archaeologists have also uncovered buildings and artifacts from this ancient community known as Qumran. Most scholars today believe that the community was an Essene sect of Judaism.

◄ **THE FAMOUS ISRAELI ARCHAEOLOGIST, YIGAEL YADIN, READS ONE OF THE DEAD SEA SCROLLS** He served as head of the Institute of Archaeology at Hebrew University and did much important work on the scrolls.

▼ **THE ENTRANCE OF CAVE 4** This cave yielded the richest deposit of manuscripts from the eleven different caves. (RIGHT) An aerial view of the site of Qumran.

◄ A pottery jar from Qumran that was used to store scrolls.

▼ **THE FAMOUS ISAIAH SCROLL FROM QUMRAN CONTAINING THE ENTIRE TEXT OF THE PROPHET (1QIsᵃ)** The complete scroll measures twenty-four feet in length. Another Isaiah scroll was discovered (1QIsᵇ) that was lengthy but fragmentary.

◀ An inkwell from the site.

THE SYSTEM OF ABBREVIATIONS USED IN CLASSIFYING THE SCROLLS

The cave where the scroll was found (1 to 11).

The "Q" designates Qumran.

The "6" is an inventory number.

11Q6 or 11QPsᵇ

The same document sometimes also has a more descriptive designation.

"Ps" is an abbreviation for "Psalms."

The superscript "b" indicates that this is the second Psalms scroll or fragment discovered in this cave.

WHAT IS THE OLD TESTAMENT?

Although "old" may imply outdated or obsolete, the Old Testament is as important today as it was centuries ago. This collection of thirty-nine books written over a span of 1,500 years not only reveals the nature and character of the one true God but also chronicles his involvement in human history. The word testament means covenant and refers to God's agreement with his people. God chose Abraham and promised to bless his descendants and make them a special people through whom he would bless all the nations of the world (Gen. 12:1–3, 15). These books record significant promises that God made. The foundational promise especially relevant to us is "the new covenant" (Jer. 31:31–34; Ezek. 36–37). Central to this covenant would be a decisive activity on God's part to deal with the problem of human sinfulness and to provide the gift of his Spirit in the lives of all his people. The Old Testament portrays God as earnestly seeking to have a relationship with his people, motivated by his great love. He is constrained, however, by the problem of human sinfulness—an affront to his holiness and purity.

▼ **A MAP OF ISRAEL SHOWING THE DIVISION OF THE LAND AMONG THE TWELVE TRIBES** These twelve represented the descendants of the sons of Jacob.

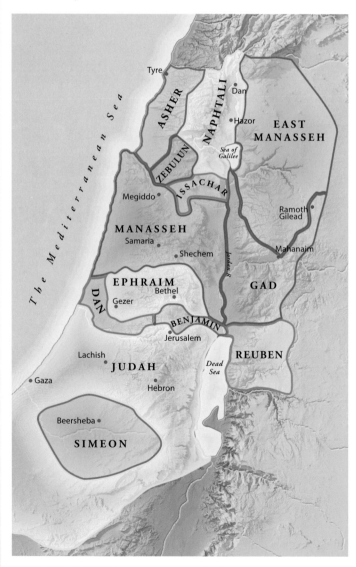

◀ **UR OF THE CHALDEES, 190 MILES SOUTHEAST OF BAGHDAD IN IRAQ** It was from this city that God called Abraham into a special relationship with himself. Abraham was the father of Isaac and Isaac was the father of Jacob (or Israel).

◀ **AN ARTISTIC REPRESENTATION OF THE TEMPLE OF SOLOMON** Built roughly a thousand years before the time of Christ, this massive structure served as a center for the worship of God. Various pilgrim festivals brought Jews from all over the world to offer sacrifice and praise to God.

◄ A TORAH SCROLL
Following the Exodus, God gave his law to the Jewish people. The law not only consisted of the Ten Commandments and other obligations, but it also established a sacrificial system. The blood of bulls and other animals was poured out as a means of reconciling God to his sinful people. These sacrifices, however, were never enough to erase the offence of sins.

THE BOOKS OF THE OLD TESTAMENT BY CONTENTS AND DATE

The Torah
Genesis, Exodus, Leviticus, Numbers, Deuteronomy
   Contents: History from Abraham to the Exodus and the law of God revealed at Sinai.
   Dates (approximate): 2100 BC to the 1300s BC

Historical Books
Joshua, Judges, Ruth, 1 Samuel, 2 Samuel, 1 Kings, 2 Kings, 1 Chronicles, 2 Chronicles
   Contents: History from the conquest of the Promised Land until the exile to Babylon.
   Dates (approximate): late 1300s to 536 BC

Character Portraits
Ezra, Nehemiah, Esther, Job
   Contents: A glimpse of Israel under Persian rule and the rebuilding of Jerusalem.
   Dates (approximate): 400s BC (Job is probably much earlier.)

The Hymn Book of Ancient Israel
Psalms
   Dates: many written by David c. 1000 BC

Wisdom Literature
Proverbs, Ecclesiastes
   Author: Solomon, King of Israel
   Dates: mid-900s BC

The Song of Solomon
   Contents: A poem describing Solomon's love for his wife.
   Dates: mid-900s BC

The Major Prophets
Isaiah, Jeremiah, Lamentations, Ezekiel, Daniel
   Contents: Prophecies of the Assyrian captivity, Babylonian captivity, as well as future events. Through them God calls his people to repentance.
   Dates: 700s to 500s BC

The Minor Prophets
Hosea, Joel, Amos, Obadiah, Jonah, Micah, Nahum, Habakkuk, Zephaniah, Haggai, Zechariah, Malachi
   Contents: God spoke to his people through these men calling them to commitment, faithfulness, and obedience.
   Dates: 800s to 400s BC

A TIMELINE OF BIBLICAL HISTORY

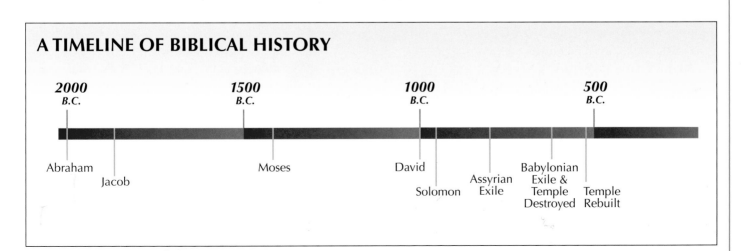

2000 B.C.	*1500* B.C.	*1000* B.C.	*500* B.C.
Abraham	Moses	David	Babylonian Exile & Temple Destroyed
Jacob		Solomon · Assyrian Exile	Temple Rebuilt

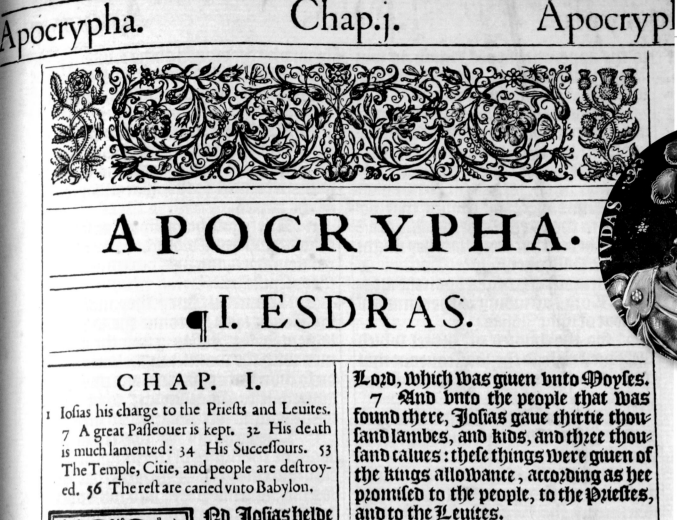

The beginning of the Apocrypha in the King James Version of 1611.

THE APOCRYPHA

The word *apocrypha* means "secret" or "hidden," yet there is nothing secret about these fifteen books. These writings were printed in the original King James Bible of 1611 and are part of all Catholic Bibles printed today. Whereas most forms of the Old Testament end with the book of Malachi, written in the fifth century BC, all of the Old Testament apocryphal books were written in the first or second century BC. They are a collection of Jewish documents that provide us with extensive information about Judaism in the two centuries leading up to the time of Christ. The Apocrypha were not regarded by the Jews, however, as part of Scripture and were thus not a part of the authoritative collection of writings (that is, the Old Testament canon). They were widely read by the Jewish and early Christian communities. The books were even included in some very important Greek manuscripts of the Old Testament. The label "apocrypha" was first applied to them by the Latin church father Jerome, who distinguished them from inspired Scripture and did not include them in the Latin Vulgate. Later editions of the Vulgate did include them, and the Western church tradition came to accept them as Scripture.

▼ **A COIN DEPICTING THE IMAGE OF ANTIOCHUS IV EPIPHANES (175–163 BC)** This king imposed Greek law and customs on the Israelites leading to the Maccabean revolt (167 BC).

MARTIN LUTHER

He included the Apocrypha in his translation of the Bible (except 1 & 2 Esdras), but as an appendix. In his preface, he says, "Apocrypha, that is, books which are not held equal to the sacred Scriptures, and nevertheless are useful and good to read."

Since the mid–1800s, few Protestant Bibles have included the Apocrypha.

◀ **JUDAS MACCABEUS** The apocryphal book known as 1 Maccabees narrates the exploits of this valiant Jewish warrior, who led Israel in a revolt against the foreign Seleucid rulers in the second century BC.

▲ The end of the book of Tobit in the fourth-century AD Codex Sinaiticus.

Characteristics of the Apocryphal Books

Historical Books

1 Esdras (or, 3 Ezra)	2c. BC	an elaboration on Ezra's religious reforms
1 Maccabees	2c. BC	a history of the Jews from Antiochus Epiphanes to John Hyrcanus (c. 175-104 BC)
2 Maccabees	1c. BC	a history of the Jews covering the mid-second century

Wisdom Literature

Ecclesiasticus (or, Wisdom of Jesus ben Sirach)	2c. BC	wisdom literature similar to Proverbs
Wisdom of Solomon	1c. BC	exhortations to wisdom and virtue
Letter of Jeremiah	2c. BC	a letter purportedly written by the prophet Jeremiah to Jewish captives about to be taken to Babylon
Baruch	2c. BC	a letter purportedly written by Baruch (Jeremiah's helper) to fellow Jews in Jerusalem during the Babylonian captivity

Apocalyptic Book

2 Esdras (4 Ezra)	1c. BC	a series of seven revelations given to Ezra by the angel Uriel regarding God's plan for the world

Miscellaneous

Tobit	2c. BC	tales involving magic and folk belief surrounding the character Tobit, an Israelite living in Nineveh
Judith	2c. BC	the story of a noble Israelite widow who slays the head of the Assyrian army
Susanna	2c. BC	tale of a woman rescued by Daniel after she refuses to have sex with two elders
The Additions to Esther (Greek version)	1c. BC	additions to the book of Esther highlighting the religious factors in the story of Esther
Bel and the Dragon	1c. BC	tales of Daniel's exploits in Babylon against idolatry
Prayer of Azaraiah and Song of Three Men	2c. BC	tales of Daniel's three companions during the episode of the fiery furnace including a hymn and a prayer
Prayer of Manasseh	1c. BC	alleged record of King Manasseh's prayer (2 Chronicles 33:10-13)

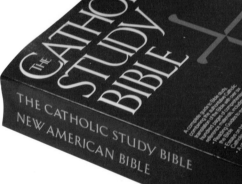

▲ **A MODERN CATHOLIC STUDY BIBLE IN THE NEW AMERICAN VERSION** The Apocryphal books are incorporated into the Old Testament of this Bible. The Roman Catholic Council of Trent (1548) confirmed the full canonicity of the books. This decision was reaffirmed by the first Vatican council (1870).

AN ANCIENT STOREROOM OF MANUSCRIPTS: THE CAIRO GENIZAH

▲ A PORTION OF A LEATHER TORAH SCROLL FROM THE CAIRO GENIZAH
The columns contain the text of Genesis 47:27–50:23. The manuscript dates to the tenth or eleventh century AD (although it could be earlier). It is designated T-S AS 37.1.

In 1896, Solomon Schechter, the famous lecturer in Talmudic studies at Cambridge University traveled to Cairo, Egypt, to examine some ancient manuscripts. Upon arriving at an old synagogue in Cairo, he gained access to the forgotten storeroom used for stowing away worn out manuscripts. This windowless and doorless room, called a *genizah,* could only be reached by climbing up a ladder and entering through a small crawlspace. In this dark and dusty room, Schechter found a priceless horde of ancient manuscripts. About 200,000 fragments have now been identified. Much of the collection was taken to the Cambridge University Library, where it is housed today. Among the materials Schechter obtained from the genizah were thirty-seven boxes with fragments of biblical texts. In addition to this were versions of the Bible, Targums, Talmuds, and a variety of other kinds of Jewish literature dating to the middle ages. There are at least sixty small fragments of biblical manuscripts that date before AD 1200, all of which attest to the Masoretic tradition (such as that found in Codex Leningradensis, upon which our Hebrew Old Testament is based).

◄ **A PAPER LEAF FROM A CODEX OF THE TORAH FROM THE PERIOD OF THE TENTH TO TWELFTH CENTURY AD** This portion contains Genesis 5:20–32. It is designated T-S AS 46.35r.

► **THE OPPOSITE SIDE (VERSO) OF THE SAME CODEX** The text depicted is Genesis 6:1–12. The manuscript is designated T-S 46.35verso.

◄ **A LEAF FROM CODEX CAIRENSIS (THE CAIRO CODEX OF THE PROPHETS) THAT DATES TO AD 895** This leaf records the text of Judges 5, the story of Deborah and Barak.

► **THE EBEN EZRAH SYNAGOGUE IN CAIRO WHERE THE FAMOUS GENIZAH WAS LOCATED** Originally the Christian Church of St. Michael, the building was sold to the Jews in AD 882 and converted into a synagogue.

AN ANCIENT REPOSITORY OF MANUSCRIPTS IN THE SINAI DESERT

In 1844, Constantine von Tischendorf travelled to an Orthodox monastery in the Sinai Desert searching for biblical manuscripts. The young University of Leipzig (Germany) scholar was planning to edit a new edition of the Greek New Testament and wanted to take into account as many manuscripts as he could identify. While staying at the monastery, he found a bin filled with leaves from a manuscript that were allegedly being used by the monks as paper to light fires. The forty-three leaves were from an Old Testament manuscript that dated to the fourth century AD. In a subsequent visit, Tischendorf discovered the entire codex of which they were a part. The codex contained most of the Old Testament, the entire New Testament, and two second-century Christian documents. This manuscript, which came to be known as codex Sinaiticus (‏א‎), is one of the two oldest complete manuscripts of the New Testament. The entire manuscript collection at St. Catherine's includes 254 New Testament manuscripts. The story is not complete, however. In 1975, workmen accidentally broke through a wall and discovered a small room with 3,000 more manuscripts, including some missing leaves from Codex Sinaiticus.

▼ **A LEAF FROM CODEX SINAITICUS** This is a leaf from the beginning of John's gospel. The codex is the only known copy of the entire New Testament in Greek uncial script (capital letters). It is also the only four-column manuscript of the NT.

▲ Constantine von Tischendorf

▲ **A CLOSE-UP VIEW OF THE WRITING STYLE OF CODEX SINAITICUS** This is John 1:1–4.

▲ **THE CEILING OF THE MANUSCRIPT STOREROOM (GENIZAH) FOUND IN THE 1975 DISCOVERY IN ST. GEORGE'S TOWER AT THE MONASTERY** The monks are using state-of-the-art digital equipment to digitize all of the 3,300 manuscripts housed at the monastery.

NOVUM TESTAMENTUM
GRAECE.

AD ANTIQUOS TESTES DENUO RECENSUIT

APPARATUM CRITICUM OMNI STUDIO PERFECTUM

APPOSUIT

COMMENTATIONEM ISAGOGICAM

PRAETEXUIT

AENOTH. FRID. CONST. TISCHENDORF

PHIL. ET THEOL. DR. THEOL. PROF. P. O. H. ORDD. REG. SAX. ALB. IMP. RUSS. S.
STAN. CL. II. IMP. FRANC. LEG. HON. REG. BOR. AQU. RUB. CL. III. REG. BAV. S. MICH.
CL. I. REG. SUEC. DE STELL. POL. REG. SARD. SS. MAUR. ET LAZ. REG. GRAEC. SALV.
DUC. PARM. S. LUD. EQUES, SOCIET. REG. SCIENT. UPSAL. PRO DEF. REL. CHR. HAG.
HIST. THEOL. LIPS. ORIENT. GERM. SOC.

EDITIO SEPTIMA.

PARS PRIOR.

LIPSIAE, SUMPTIBUS ADOLPHI WINTER.

1859.

▶ A copy of the Greek New Testament edited by Tischendorf.

ST. CATHERINE'S MONASTERY

This Greek Orthodox monastery was built in AD 527 on the site where they presumed Moses encountered the burning bush.

▲ The 1903 excavations at the site of Oxyrhynchus, Egypt.

EARLY PAPYRUS TEXTS OF THE NEW TESTAMENT

Beginning in the late 1800s, a series of highly important manuscript discoveries were made in the sands of Egypt. These papyrus texts, preserved by the arid desert climate, dated as early as the second century AD with most stemming from the third and fourth century. Their significance lies in the fact that they pre-dated the earliest manuscripts used for the Bibles of the early 1800s by more than 700 years. The first to come to light was a portion of Luke's gospel discovered in Coptos, Egypt in 1889 that dated to AD 200 (now designated $\mathfrak{P}^4$). Then, in 1897, B. P. Grenfell and A. S. Hunt found a fragment of the New Testament near a village on the upper Nile named Oxyrhynchus, a place that would eventually yield thousands of papyrus documents of all kinds, including many more New Testament fragments. The number of known papyrus texts of the New Testament increased from nine in 1900 to forty in the 1930s. That number has now increased to 115 with the likelihood that even more will be discovered. In addition to New Testament texts, numerous fragments of the Greek Old Testament have also been discovered.

▼ A third-century fragment of Hebrews 1:7–12 designated $\mathfrak{P}^{114}$. This text was found at Oxyrhynchus and published in 1999.

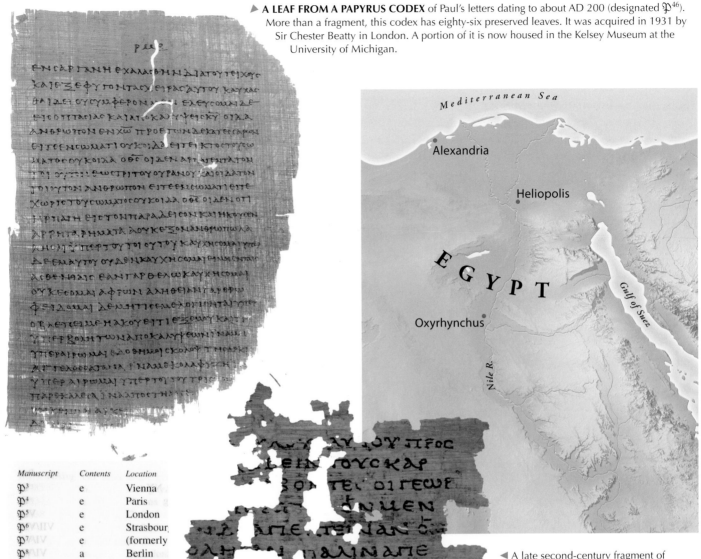

▶ **A LEAF FROM A PAPYRUS CODEX** of Paul's letters dating to about AD 200 (designated $\mathfrak{P}^{46}$). More than a fragment, this codex has eighty-six preserved leaves. It was acquired in 1931 by Sir Chester Beatty in London. A portion of it is now housed in the Kelsey Museum at the University of Michigan.

◀ A late second-century fragment of Matthew 21 designated $\mathfrak{P}^{104}$. This text was found at Oxyrhynchus.

Manuscript	Contents	Location
$\mathfrak{P}^3$	e	Vienna
$\mathfrak{P}^4$	e	Paris
$\mathfrak{P}^5$	e	London
$\mathfrak{P}^6$	e	Strasbour
$\mathfrak{P}^7$	e	(formerly
$\mathfrak{P}^8$	a	Berlin
$\mathfrak{P}^9$	c	Cambridg
$\mathfrak{P}^{10}$	p	Cambridg

▲ **A LIST OF ANCIENT PAPYRI** taken into account in the creation of a modern edition of the Greek New Testament published by the United Bible Societies. The symbol used in designating them is a gothic $\mathfrak{P}$.

THE PUBLISHED OXYRHYNCHUS

volumes, in addition to the publication of all other papryi, are available for anyone to inspect in most research libraries.

NEW TESTAMENT

...*erlieferung* I (1972 ed. revised by K. Aland). I ha... ...ce on the collating from the Rev. Dr David Parke... ...s follow the practice of Nestle-Aland[27].

4401. MATTHEW III 10–12; III 16–IV 3

4.7 × 8.6 cm

...is broken away on all four sides; the restorations ...trary. The lines on both sides contain between 18... ↓ and →, assuming a standard text, amounts... ...lines (in addition to the two lines partially prese... ...32 or 33 lines per page, which would give a wr...

▲ **WHEN A PAPYRUS TEXT IS DISCOVERED,** a scholar carefully studies the document and writes a detailed report for publication. The analysis also contains photographs of the document and a transcription of the text. This is a sample page from the 1997 publication of a third-century papyrus fragment of Matthew 3.

EARLY PARCHMENT MANUSCRIPTS OF THE BIBLE

The most important manuscripts of the New Testament known today are written on parchment (or vellum) and date to the fourth and fifth centuries AD. Two of these manuscripts, Sinaiticus (א) and Vaticanus (B), did not come to light until the mid- to late 1800s. They played a significant role in prompting the revision of the King James Bible. The early parchment manuscripts are written in the same style of script as the New Testament papyri. They both em-

ploy an "uncial" (capital letters) form of writing and are thus sometimes called uncial manuscripts. There are about three hundred uncial manuscripts of the New Testament, yet only eighteen of these have more than thirty pages. They range in date from the third to the eleventh century AD.

◄ **A LEAF FROM CODEX VATICANUS (B)** It is a fourth-century manuscript containing the complete Bible. It is housed in the Vatican library in Rome. The early history of this manuscript is unknown. The oldest reference to it is in a Vatican inventory in 1475, but it was not used for Bible translation purposes until the late 1800s. It is here opened to John 16.

▲ **BROOKE FOSS WESTCOTT (1825–1901), BISHOP OF DURHAM AND PROFESSOR AT CAMBRIDGE UNIVERSITY** His understanding of the history of the text of the Greek New Testament had a profound influence on Bible translation.

CHART OF THE UNCIAL MANUSCRIPTS BY CENTURY

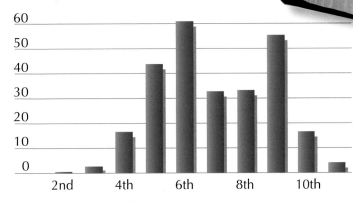

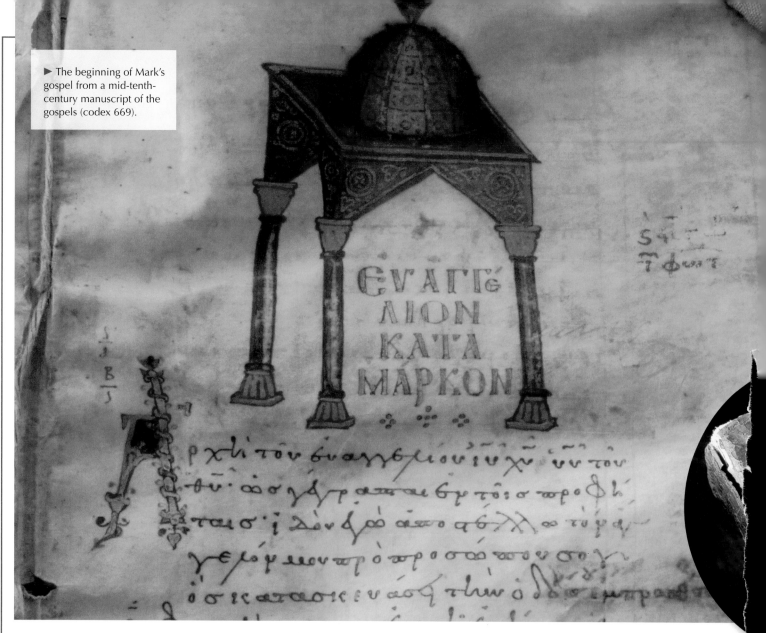

ϵΥΑΓΓ
ΛΙΟΝ
ΚΑΤΑ
ΜΑΡΚΟΝ

5,000 GREEK MANUSCRIPTS FROM THE MIDDLE AGES

The bulk of the 5,500 Greek manuscripts of the New Testament are parchments that use a minuscule (or cursive) script. This style of writing made its debut in the ninth century AD and continued in use for centuries. Most of the minuscule manuscripts date to the Middle Ages, particularly the tenth through the fifteenth centuries, until the invention of the printing press. Even after that, however, scribes and monks continued to make parchment copies of the New Testament by hand. Almost all of the minuscule manuscripts of this age tend to reflect one textual family known as the Byzantine, or Majority, text. In other words, they usually agree with one another against other forms of the text (such as the papyri) when there are variations. Most scholars conjecture that a standardized form of the Greek text was created in the fourth or fifth century AD after Christianity had become a legalized religion in the empire and there were no more book burnings and much less persecution. The minuscule manuscripts are probably copies of this "authorized" form of the text.

▶ A minuscule manuscript of Acts and the Epistles that dates to AD 1107.

A SAMPLE VARIATION BETWEEN TEXTUAL FAMILIES: LUKE 24:53

"And they were continually in the temple . . . "

" . . . blessing (*eulogountes*) God."	*Alexandrian* family of manuscripts (e.g. Sinaiticus, Vaticanus, an early papyrus)
" . . . praising (*ainountes*) God."	*Western* family of manuscripts (e.g. Bezae, Old Latin manuscripts)
" . . . blessing and praising (*eulogountes kai ainountes*) God."	*Byzantine* family of manuscripts (e.g. nearly all of the miniscule manuscripts)

▲ One of the reasons scholars such as Westcott viewed the Byzantine form of the text as less reliable than the Alexandrian form is because of the presence of "conflate" readings. This is where it appears that a later scribe has *combined* two different manuscript readings as in this example from Luke's gospel.

▲ A thirteenth-century codex of the gospels (codex 2813).

◄ A codex manuscript of the gospels from the ninth century AD.

▲ **THE HAGIA SOPHIA IN ISTANBUL, TURKEY** For 1,000 years it was the "cathedral of the ecumenical patriarchate of Constantinople." Planned by the emperor Justinian, the "holy wisdom" church was completed on December 27, 537. Constantinople was the capital of the Byzantine empire and the place where numerous minuscule manuscripts were made.

CHART OF THE DISTRIBUTION OF NEW TESTAMENT MINUSCULE MANUSCRIPTS BY CENTURY

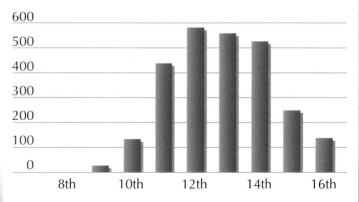

A page from an AD 1225 copy of the Latin Vulgate with a beautiful illumination

◄ **A LEAF FROM A THIRTEENTH-CENTURY MANUSCRIPT OF THE LATIN VULGATE** There are over 10,000 manuscripts of the Latin Vulgate that still survive.

THE BIBLE IS TRANSLATED INTO LATIN

As Christianity made deeper inroads into the Latin-speaking Roman world, believers wanted to hear and read the Bible in their own language. Latin was spoken in Italy, North Africa, and in various Roman colonies scattered throughout the Mediterranean world. No one knows when the first Latin translation of the Scriptures was produced, but it probably took place in the mid- to late second century AD, if not before. From that point on, so many different translations of the Scriptures into Latin were made that the western church father Augustine (AD 354–430) complained of their extraordinary number. The problem was that many of the translations were done without proper caution and care. This led Pope Damasus (AD 366–384) to commission the brightest Hebrew, Greek, and Latin scholar of his day to produce an authorized form of the Latin text that would remedy this problem and bring the text back into the closest possible conformity with the original. This scholar, Sophronius Eusebius Hieronymus (or Jerome) worked hard to produce his edition of the Latin text that became known as the Vulgate. "Vulgate" comes from the Latin word, *vulgare*, and refers to the common speech of the people. It highlights Jerome's desire to create a readable and understandable translation.

◄ A close-up of the upper left corner of the Vulgate manuscript from AD 1280.

▲ A page from a Latin Vulgate dating to AD 1280.

◀ AN ARTISTIC RENDITION OF JEROME BY GEORGES DE LA TOUR (1593–1652) Jerome completed his translation of the Bible in the late fourth century AD.

◀ AN ILLUMINATION OF THE SCRIBE EZRA The image is from Codex Amiatanus, an eighth century AD manuscript of the entire Latin Bible. This codex is regarded as the most reliable form of the Latin Vulgate text. It was made in the north of England at Wearmouth and Jarrow.

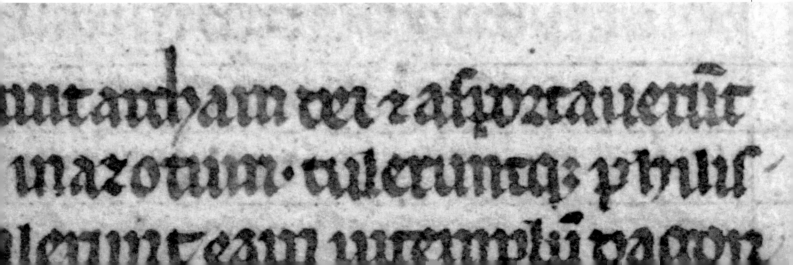

THE LARGEST AND HEAVIEST MANUSCRIPT OF THE BIBLE

The biggest manuscript of the Bible, appropriately named "Codex Gigas" (from which we get the word "gigantic"), weighs 165 pounds and measures 49 x 89.5 cm (20" x 36"). It was copied in the thirteenth century in the Benedictine monastery of Podlažice in Bohemia. It is said to have taken the skins of 160 donkeys to supply enough parchment. The text is of the Latin vulgate. The manuscript is also called "the Devil's Bible" not only because it contains a large illumination of the devil, but also due to a legend attached to the Bible.

According to the story, the scribe was a monk who violated some rule of the monastery and, as a consequence, was confined to his cell. As penance for his misdeed, the scribe completed the manuscript in one night with the assistance of the Devil, who he called upon to provide him with assistance. This manuscript is currently housed in the Royal Library of Stockholm, Sweden.

▼ ► The cover of and an illumination from Codex Gigas.

▲ A page from Codex Gigas.

► By contrast to Codex Gigas, this is a page from a 1919 miniature Bible. This page is not much wider than the sharpened portion of a pencil.

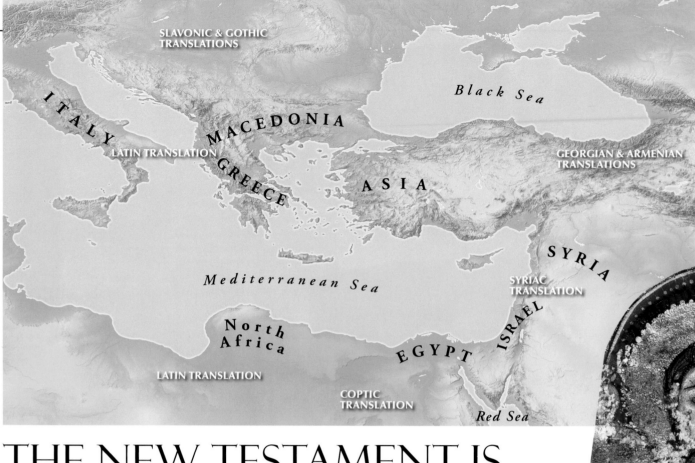

SLAVONIC & GOTHIC
TRANSLATIONS

Black Sea

ITALY

MACEDONIA

LATIN TRANSLATION

GREECE

ASIA

GEORGIAN & ARMENIAN
TRANSLATIONS

Mediterranean Sea

SYRIA

SYRIAC
TRANSLATION

North
Africa

ISRAEL

EGYPT

LATIN TRANSLATION

COPTIC
TRANSLATION

Red Sea

THE NEW TESTAMENT IS TRANSLATED INTO OTHER LANGUAGES

After Jesus rose from the dead and before he ascended to heaven, he told his disciples that they would soon receive the Holy Spirit and "be my witnesses in Jerusalem, and in all Judea and Samaria, and to the ends of the earth" (Acts 1:8). What Jesus said quickly became true, and Christianity spread throughout the Mediterranean world and far beyond. As churches were established in many different lands among a variety of different people groups, there was a desire for the Scripture to be available in the native languages of the people. Translations of the New Testament were carried out in languages such as Latin, Ethiopic, Coptic, Slavonic, Armenian, Syriac, and many others.

Today we have numerous ancient manuscript copies of the New Testament in these languages. Some of them date as early as the third and fourth centuries AD.

◀ A COPY OF THE GOSPELS IN SLAVONIC DATING TO THE SIXTEENTH CENTURY AD There is evidence of Slavic peoples becoming Christians as early as the sixth century AD.

▲ A COPY OF THE NEW TESTAMENT TRANSLATED INTO SYRIAC THAT DATES TO THE SIXTH CENTURY AD The New Testament describes the introduction of Christianity into the city of Antioch in Syria (Acts 11:19–30). Although Greek was spoken in Antioch, Syriac was the language of the people of the land.

◄ An illumination of Peter and Paul from an Armenian manuscript dating to AD 1279.

DECORATIVE COVER TO A 1659 COPY OF THE GOSPELS IN ARMENIAN ▾

Although we do not know the details of the beginnings of Christianity in Armenia, the historian Eusebius reports that the church was already established there by the middle of the third century AD.

◄ An illumination from a leaf of an Armenian manuscript dating to AD 1121.

AN ETHIOPIC COPY OF THE GOSPELS FROM THE EIGHTEENTH CENTURY AD

The oldest Ethiopic manuscript known dates to the tenth century AD. The book of Acts in the New Testament narrates the story of a government official from Ethiopia becoming a Christian in the mid-first century AD (Acts 8:26–40).

WHAT IS THE NEW TESTAMENT?

The foundational promise God made through the prophets and recorded in the Old Testament is the promise of a *new covenant,* or *new testament* (Jer. 31:31–34; Ezek. 36–37). Central to this covenant would be a decisive activity on God's part to deal with the problem of human sinfulness. This happened in the death of Jesus Christ upon the cross. In the horror and suffering on the cross, Jesus absorbed God's wrath against sin in his own body and in our place. Much of the New Testament describes the passion of Christ and reflects on its significance for us. When Jesus of Nazareth began his three-year public ministry, he announced that he had come in fulfillment of this new covenant promise. During the last supper as he distributed the bread and wine to his disciples, he remarked, "This cup is the *new covenant* in my blood, which is poured out for you" (Luke 22:20). Jesus was truly "the lamb of God who takes away the sin of the world" (John 1:29). The twenty-seven books of the New Testament provide testimony of God's work in and through Jesus to fulfill this new covenant promise. They also speak about the gift of God's Spirit to his people. The Holy Spirit is the personal, empowering presence of God in the lives of Christians.

▲ **AN ELEVENTH-CENTURY ANGLO-SAXON RELIEF MADE FROM WALRUS IVORY** Christ is here depicted in majesty after his resurrection. He embraces the Scripture in his left hand. The New Testament teaches that Jesus is alive, currently reigning as Lord over his church, and will return again to the earth in triumph over evil.

▶ A list of the books of the New Testament from the table of contents in a Matthew's Bible (1537).

▶ **AN ILLUMINATION FROM A TWELFTH-CENTURY LATIN VULGATE** The bottom panel depicts life under the old covenant when priests needed to sacrifice animals on the altar for forgiveness of sins. The top panel depicts the once-and-for-all sacrifice of Christ, the only sacrifice that can truly bring forgiveness of sins and reconciliation to God.

THE BOOKS OF THE NEW TESTAMENT BY CONTENTS AND DATE

The Gospels
Matthew, Mark, Luke, John

Contents: Each provide an account of what Jesus taught and did during his three-year ministry. Foremost, however, is their narration of Jesus' suffering, death, and resurrection

Dates: Matthew, Mark, and Luke were written in the period AD 55–68. John's gospel was witten in the 90s.

Acts

Contents: An account of the history of Christianity from the resurrection of Jesus to the apostle Paul's imprisonment in Rome covering AD 30–62. The book describes the coming of the Holy Spirit at Pentecost, Peter's preaching and the growth of the church in Jerusalem, the persecution of Jewish Christians and their scattering, the spread of the gospel to non-Jews residing in Syria, Asia Minor, Greece, and Rome, and the Apostle Paul's role in starting churches.

Dates: mid-60s

The Pauline Epistles
Romans, 1 & 2 Corinthians, Galatians, Ephesians, Philippians, Colossians, 1& 2 Thessalonians, 1 & 2 Timothy, Titus, Philemon

Contents: Thirteen letters written by the Apostle Paul: Nine to churches and four to people. The letters show Paul's deep pastoral concern for the churches and his attempt to assist them in their growth. They are rich with teaching about knowing God, having a relationship with Christ, how to overcome in the struggle with sin, and much more.

Dates: The earliest letter (Galatians) was written around AD 49. Paul's last letter (2 Timothy) was written around AD 65.

The General Epistles
Hebrews, James, 1 & 2 Peter, 1, 2, & 3 John, Jude

Contents: Letters to churches by five different people. Hebrews has much to say about Christ as our "High Priest." James is a book of practical wisdom for day-to-day living. Peter's letters were written to a group of Christians who were suffering and facing great difficulties. 1 John says much about knowing Christ and what that means for daily living.

Dates: The earliest letter (James) was written in the mid-40s. John's letters were the latest, written in the 90s.

The Apocalypse (or Revelation)

Contents: A detailed account of a "revelation" or vision given to the Apostle John. The vision was given during the reign of the emporor Domitian (AD 81–96) who demanded that his subjects address him as "lord and God" and worship his image. The book is largely a prophecy about God's future triumph over all evil. Revelation has provided comfort and hope to many Christians throughout the centuries, but it has also been misinterpreted and misused by charlatans with often disastrous consequences.

Dates: mid-90s

▲ A REPRESENTATION OF JESUS CHRIST FROM THE BOOK OF KELLS Jesus is here depicted holding the Scripture close to his side.

ILLUMINATED MANUSCRIPTS

During the Middle Ages, some scribes began to adorn manuscripts with artwork. This extended from decorated capital letters at the beginning of a line to elaborate depictions of biblical scenes. The earliest known illuminated manuscript is the sixth-century Codex Rossanensis, which contains seventeen illustrations in watercolors. One of the most dazzling and magnificent illuminated manuscripts is the book of Kells. This 680-page manuscript of the Latin text of the four gospels contains colorful and brilliant ornamentation on every page. Produced in the eighth or ninth century in the Kells monastery (County Meath, Ireland), the manuscript reflects virtually thousands of hours of careful work done to the glory of God in appreciation for his Word. The artwork consists of many intricate shapes and patterns in the typical Celtic style.

GOSPEL SYMBOLS

The symbols of the four evangelists in the Book of Kells: the man for Matthew (the humanity of Christ), the lion for Mark (Christ's resurrection), the ox for Luke (Christ's sacrifice), and the eagle for John (Christ's divinity). The inspiration for the symbols may have come from Ezekiel's vision of the four living creatures (Ezekiel 1).

▶ THE SYMBOL OF MARK'S GOSPEL A Depiction of a lion, from the Book of Durrow. This manuscript is a predecessor to the book of Kells and was produced either in Ireland or Northumbria in the second half of the seventh century AD. The book of Kells employs a similar style of Celtic art.

▲ CODEX PURPUREUS ROSSANENSIS (CODEX Σ) The leaf here depicts Jesus standing before Pilate (top panel) and the repentance and death of Judas (bottom panel).

◀ AN ARTISTIC REPRESENTATION OF THE NAME "MATTHEW" AT THE BEGINNING OF THE BOOK OF KELLS The blue (ultramarine) color was derived from lapis lazuli that came from Afghanistan.

▲ AN ILLUMINATION OF LUKE, the author of the third gospel and the book of Acts. This is from a twelfth-century Greek manuscript (Codex 163) housed in the National Library of Athens.

SCRIBES AND SCRIPTORIA

▲ THE BEAUTIFUL SETTING OF THE GREGORIOU MONASTERY AT MOUNT ATHOS, GREECE
There are twenty monasteries at Mount Athos that have been there since the Byzantine era.

Before the invention of the printing press in AD 1454, all books were copied by hand. This was a long, laborious, and expensive process. In the centuries before Christ, the scribes responsible for copying the Hebrew Bible were called *sopherim.* This Hebrew term, meaning "to count," points to the care with which the early scribes took in copying each word of the Scripture because they used to count all the letters to insure none were added or left out. This procedure continued with the Masoretes who kept detailed word statistics for the same purpose. Scribes who copied the Greek New Testament also took great care. In the first four centuries of the church, before Christianity was a legal religion, copies were probably made on an individual basis. After the legalization of Christianity by the emperor Constantine, special rooms, called *scriptoria*, were often used for scribal work. In these, multiple copies could be made from a single exemplar, which was read aloud to the scribes seated at desks in the room. From the eleventh century AD on almost every abbey and monastery had its own scriptorium.

► Archaeologists have identified this portion of a building at Qumran as the Scriptorium where the Dead Sea Scrolls were produced.

◄ **THE TEXT OF EPHESIANS 1:1 IN CODEX SINAITICUS** Notice the following characteristics:
- Scribes would often abbreviate the divine names by taking the first and last letter and drawing a line over them.
- Later scribes would occasionally make corrections to the text. In this case, the scribe inserted the words "in Ephesus" to the left margin.

ABBREVIATIONS OF DIVINE NAMES IN EPHESIANS 1:1

Abbrev.	Greek Word	Translation
ΙΥ	*iēsou*	"Jesus"
ΧΥ	*christou*	"Christ"
ΘΥ	*theou*	"God"

◄ The courtyard of the Iviron Monastery on Mount Athos, Greece.

► **AN ILLUMINATION FROM A FIFTEENTH-CENTURY MANUSCRIPT COMPLETED AT THE MONASTERY OF IVIRON ON MOUNT ATHOS** Over 900 Greek New Testament manuscripts are in the collection at Mount Athos (including the important codexes Ψ, Ω, H, 1071, 1739).

ÞIHSXPS· Matheus homo

incipit euangelii
genelogia mathei

incipit argumentum ·Z·

MAR
cus

incipit euangelii

geliste di apostoli inbap

usinate filius air: incipii

▲ A LATIN-ENGLISH INTERLINEAR TRANSLATION FROM THE TENTH CENTURY AD
This is the beginning of Mark in the Lindisfarne Gospels, a Latin version completed in AD 698. Over 200 years later, a priest named Aldred added an English translation above every line.

◄ CAEDMON, who lived in the mid-seventh century on the Yorkshire coast in England, produced the earliest English form of the Bible. He took portions of the Latin Vulgate and crafted them into songs for the benefit of the common people. This stained glass representation of him is from the Kirkby Malham Church in Yorkshire.

◄ The beginning of Matthew in the Lindisfarne Gospels

THE EARLIEST ENGLISH TRANSLATIONS

Although no English translation of the entire Bible was completed until the time of John Wycliffe in the fourteenth century, a few Christian leaders did attempt to translate portions of the Bible into English. The earliest known project was undertaken by a commoner employed as a herdsman who took passages of Scripture and rendered them into beautiful vernacular songs. Inspired by a dream, Caedmon was assisted by educated monks who would recite and explain passages of Scripture to him that he would then use as the basis for his songs. A variety of other passages from the Bible were translated into English by people such as Bede, Alcuin, Alfred the Great, Aldred, and Aelfric. There were enormous constraints, however, on Christians who wanted to put the Scripture into the language of the people. Church leaders were exceedingly fearful that the commoners would misinterpret and corrupt the teaching of the Bible. Some also feared losing authority over the people and possibly also revenue. These early luminaries who ventured to bring the Scriptures to the people, however, served as a powerful inspiration to John Wycliffe.

▲ Lindisfarne Castle in Northumberland, England.

◄ **THE VENERABLE BEDE** (AD 673–735) has been lauded as the foremost scholar of Anglo-Saxon England. In addition to writing a monumental history of England, he translated the gospel of John into English.

OLD ENGLISH MANUSCRIPT

This manuscript of three long poems relates stories from Genesis, Exodus, and Daniel. It has been attributed to Caedmon, but this is doubted by some scholars. Designated Junius II, the manuscript dates to AD 1000 and is housed in the Bodleian Library, Oxford. The illumination depicts Adam and Eve in the garden.

◄ **ALFRED THE GREAT** (AD 849–899) was a famous English monarch who sought to remedy England's degeneracy by promoting a revival of learning. He translated many works into English, including a few small portions of the Bible.

► **AN OXFORDSHIRE CLERGYMAN** by the name of Aelfric (AD 955–1020) translated portions of the first seven books of the Bible into English. This is a page from his Heptateuch with illustrations of the Israelites' flight from Egypt.

ALL

THE FIRST COMPLETE BIBLE IN ENGLISH: THE WYCLIFFE BIBLE

◄ The prologue to Matthew's gospel from an original edition of the Wycliffe Bible.

John Wycliffe (1330–1384), a reformer of the church before the Reformation, lived at a time when the corruption of the church was descending to murkier depths. Reaching the limits of his tolerance, Wycliffe spoke out sharply against the depravity in the church and some of its doctrines not rooted in Scripture. Because of his passionate efforts, historians have referred to this Oxford professor as "the Morning Star of the Reformation." Above all, and certainly foundational to his reforms, was a belief in the authority of Scripture over tradition and the right of every person, including the common people, to read and interpret the Bible. In fact, Wycliffe wrote a 1,000-page book on the value and authority of the Bible entitled *The Truth of Scripture*. The crowning work of his life, however, was a translation of the entire Bible into English. With substantial help from his colleague, Nicholas Purvey, the project was completed in 1382 and based upon the Latin Vulgate. Although many English people received the new Bible gladly, Pope John XXIII condemned it, referring to the man behind it as "this pestilent and wretched John Wyclif, of cursed memory, that son of the old serpent."

▲ A portrait of John Wycliffe

◄ The beginning of Mark's gospel in a Wycliffe Bible.

▼ ST. PAUL'S CATHEDRAL, LONDON John Wycliffe was condemned here in 1377.

◄ A COMPLETE WYCLIFFE BIBLE Only 170 copies of this Bible survive and only 25 of the 1382 original.

THE INVENTION OF PRINTING: THE GUTENBERG PRESS

Prior to 1454, professional scribes invested hundreds of hours in the painstaking task of making copies of the Bible by hand. Johannes Gutenberg forever changed this centuries-long tradition by creating a mechanical printing press. He devised a technique for putting movable type characters into a tray, or galley. Then, applying ink to the tray of characters, he used a press to push a piece of paper or vellum onto the block of type. Numerous copies of a page could now be made rapidly. From his shop in Mainz, Germany,

Gutenberg initially made about 180 copies of the Bible in Latin of which nearly fifty survive. He also printed a Psalter and indulgence documents for the Roman Catholic church. In the decades that followed, numerous printing presses were developed throughout the continent.

◄ **AN ENTIRE GUTENBERG BIBLE PRINTED IN 1455** The text is the Latin Vulgate.

► The Mainz Cathedral in Germany

◄ A picture of a Gutenberg press from the Gutenberg Museum in Mainz, Germany.

▼ A portrait of Johannes Gutenberg

▼ The beginning of the book of Daniel in a Gutenberg Bible.

A PRINTED INDULGENCE (MAY 3, 1508)

This sheet extends an indulgence to those who shall contribute to the building of St. Peter's at Rome. An "indulgence" represented the remission of punishment for a sin.

◄ **A PAGE FROM A GUTENBERG BIBLE** The text was printed by the mechanical press, but all of the illuminations were added by an artist.

"I totally disagree with those who are unwilling that the Holy Scriptures should be translated into everyday languages and read by unlearned people. Christ wishes his mysteries to be made known as widely as possible. I would wish even all women to read the Gospels, and the letters of St. Paul. I wish that they were translated into all the languages of all Christian people—that they might be read and known not just by the Scots and Irish, but even by the Turks and Saracens. I wish that the farm laborer might sing parts of them at his plow, that the weaver might hum them at his shuttle, and that the traveler might ease his weariness by reciting them."

▲ A portrait of Desiderius Erasmus by Hans Holbein (c. 1523).

THE FIRST PUBLISHED GREEK NEW TESTAMENT

Prior to the invention of the printing press, every copy of the Greek New Testament was written out by hand, usually in the scriptorium of a monastery. In 1516, the famed Renaissance scholar Desiderius Erasmus (1496–1536) published the first edition of a Greek New Testament. The new marvels of printing enabled Erasmus's printer, Johann Froben, to make 3,300 copies of this 1,000-page folio volume by the end of its second printing in 1519. In producing this text, Erasmus made use of six Greek manuscripts, all dating from the twelfth century and later. This was a significant advance on any other copy of the Greek New Testament, but it fell short of taking into account other older manuscripts (such as the uncial manuscripts) and the Greek papyri, which had not yet been discovered. The impact of Erasmus's Greek Text was extraordinary. It became the basis for subsequent editions of the Greek New Testament edited by Stephanus, Beza, and Elzevir. These texts became known at the "Textus Receptus," meaning, "the commonly received text" or "standard text." This form of the text lies behind the King James Version of 1611.

◀ **THE TEXT OF 1 JOHN 5:7–8,** the so-called *Comma Johanneum,* from a 1551 edition. Erasmus promised to include this Trinitarian statement if it could be found in any Greek version (it did appear in the Vulgate). The statement reads, "For there are three that bear record in heaven, the Father, the Word, and the Holy Ghost: and these three are one. And there are three that bear witness in earth …" Someone did show him a Greek manuscript that contained it, but it appears that it was copied in 1520 for this very purpose!

▼ **THE TEXT OF ROMANS 1 IN ERASMUS'S GREEK NEW TESTAMENT**
This is a diglot text with Greek on the left and his own translation into classical Latin on the right.

▼ **THE TEXT OF ACTS**
1 in an edition of the Greek New Testament edited by Robert Estienne, or Stephanus. This is a 1550, third edition, of the text.

▶ **A PAGE FROM A TWELFTH-CENTURY MINUSCULE CODEX**
that was the oldest manuscript that Erasmus used in creating his Greek New Testament. The manuscript is housed in the University Library in Basel, Switzerland, and is designated "manuscript 1." This page is the beginning of the book of Hebrews.

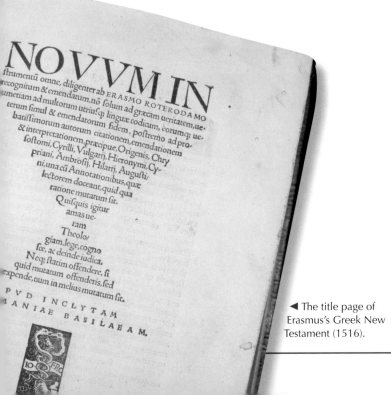

◀ The title page of Erasmus's Greek New Testament (1516).

HISTORY OF THE GREEK NEW TESTAMENT

Numerous individual manuscripts (1st century A.D. through 1500)

Erasmus (1516) ——————————— TRANSLATIONS
- based on 6 manuscripts dating from AD 1000 and later
- 5 editions

Complutensian Polyglot (1517)
Cardinal Francisco Ximines de Cisneros   **Luther** (1521)
- Done in Complutum (Alcala), Spain   (German Bible)
- Based on a few Byzantine manuscripts

Stephanus (1546) *Robert Estienne*
- based on 5th edition of Erasmus and Complutensian Polyglot
- 15 manuscripts (including D and L)

Beza (1565) ——————————————— TRANSLATIONS
- essentially the text of Stephanus (5th ed. of Erasmus)
- Made some use of 10 additional   **King James
  manuscripts (including D and Syriac)   Version** (1611)
                                                             (German Bible)
Elzevir (1624)
- essentially the text of Beza (based on Stephanus and Erasmus)
- "Here is a text received by all"

United Bible Societies (1993) ———————— TRANSLATIONS
- takes into account 5000+ Greek   **All Contemporary
  manuscripts, all the recently discovered   Versions**
  papyri, 10,000+ Latin manuscripts, all   *(except King James)*
  versions, and quotations in Church Fathers

WILLIAM TYNDALE (1494–1536) AND THE TYNDALE BIBLE

Nearly 150 years after John Wycliffe, William Tyndale followed in his steps and created a new translation of the Bible into English. Tyndale enjoyed two distinct advantages. First, thousands of copies of Tyndale's Bible could be made because of the recent invention of printing. His Bible thus has the distinction of being the first printed English Bible. Second, Tyndale was able to base his translation on the Greek New Testament recently published by Erasmus. Like Wycliffe, Tyndale was anguished over the corruption in the church and deeply concerned about the biblical illiteracy of his day, not only among the laity, but even among the clergy. He was convinced that the only hope for the church and for British society was for people to become acquainted with the Word of God. Tyndale undertook his translation work under great personal risk and sacrifice. Because it was illegal for him to carry out his activities in England, Tyndale traveled to Germany to make his translation. When the first printing was completed in 1526, the only way to get the Bibles into England was to smuggle them in by hiding them in bales of cotton and other containers. The Bishop of London violently opposed Tyndale by gathering and burning as many of the Bibles as he could find. In 1536, ten years after the publication of his Bible, Tyndale was found guilty of heresy and executed.

WILLIAM TINDALL

The newe Testament/dyly gently corrected and compared with the Greke by Willyam Tindale: and fynesshed in the yere of oure Lorde God. A. M. D. & xxxiiij. in the moneth of Nouember.

▲ A portrait of William Tyndale that appeared next to the title page of his 1534 New Testament.

◀ An illustration of the altar of incense from the Tyndale Bible.

▼ **AN ILLUSTRATION OF THE PRIESTLY EPHOD ON AARON** from the Tyndale Bible. Tyndale's translation of the Old Testament was based on the Hebrew Bible.

▼ An artistic depiction of the martyrdom and burning of William Tyndale from *The Acts and Monuments of John Foxe.*

▼ The beginning of Paul's letter to the Romans in a 1534 edition of the Tyndale New Testament.

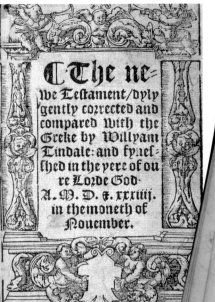

The epistle of the Apostle S. Paul to the Romayns.

The fyrst Chapter.

Paul the seruaunt of Jesus Christ / called to be an Apostle / put a parte to preache the the Gospell of God / which he promysed afore by his Prophetes / in the holy scriptures that make mension of his sonne / the seed of David / as pertayninge to the flesshe: which was begotte of the which are Jesus christes by vocacio / is declared to be the sonne of God with power of the holy goost that sanctifieth / sence the tyme that Jesus Christ oure Lorde rose agayne from deeth / by whom we have receaved grace and apostlesshyppe / to bringe all maner hethe people vnto obedience of the fayth / that is in his name: of the which hethen are ye a part also / which are Jesus christes by vocacio. To all you of Rome beloved of God and saynctes by callinge. Grace be with you and peace from God oure father / & from the Lorde Jesus Christ.

Fyrst verely I thanke my God thorow Jesus Christ for you all / because youre fayth is publisshed through out all the worlde. for God is my witnes / whom I serve with my sprete in the Gospell of his sonne / that with out

MARTIN LUTHER TRANSLATES THE BIBLE FOR THE GERMAN PEOPLE

Stricken by the weight and burden of his sinfulness, even as a scrupulous monk, Martin Luther (1483–1546) found great relief and joy in the good news of the gospel. Through his careful reading of key sections of the Bible, Luther discovered that a person could never attain the kind of righteousness that God would require for salvation through moral achievement; it could only be received as a free gift from God. As Luther reflected on this great truth, he despaired that much of the church had fallen into the wrong belief that salvation could be earned through amassing good works. These convictions became the catalyst for the Reformation. Luther soon became convinced that the German people should have direct access to this great news in the Bible in their own language, especially since none of the laity knew Latin. Luther then set out to translate the Bible from the original languages into clear, readable German. He completed the New Testament in 1522, based on the second edition of Erasmus's Greek text, and the Old Testament in 1534.

▲ The parish church at Wittenberg where Martin Luther preached.

► An illumination from a 1562 edition of the Luther Bible.

▼ **LUTHER'S ZEAL** for the contemporary value of the Bible led him to the conclusion that the Scriptures must be preached. The Bible is not simply history, but good news for the present.

▼ **THE TEXT OF ISAIAH 53 FROM A 1562 EDITION OF A LUTHER BIBLE** According to Luther, *Christ crucified* is at the heart of the Scripture and should be a constant reference point for Bible reading and preaching.

DIE BIBEL

NACH MARTIN LUTHERS ÜBERSETZUNG NEU BEARBEITET UND

DEUTSCHE BIBELGESELLSCHAFT

▲ A contemporary Luther Bible published by the German Bible Society.

◄ Portrait of Martin Luther by Lucas Cranach (1529).

THE TITLE PAGE TO A 1534 LUTHER BIBLE

In the first forty years after the publication of this Bible, over 100,000 copies were sold—an enormous amount for that time. Luther never received a penny for his work on the Bible. Numerous woodcuts depicting biblical scenes adorned the pages of the Luther Bible.

BIBLE TRANSLATIONS DURING THE REIGN OF HENRY VIII

A flurry of English Bibles were produced during the reign of Henry VIII (1509–1547), even though he did not start out supportive of these vernacular translations. In fact, he was on the throne when Tyndale faced the violent opposition that led to his martyrdom. But Henry had a change of heart after 1534. This was the year that he broke off his relationship to the Roman church and declared himself the head of the new Church of England (the Anglican church). The well-known precipitating event was the pope's denial of Henry's request to dissolve his marriage to Catherine of Aragon so he could be free to marry Anne Boleyn. In the following year, a colleague of Tyndale's named Miles Coverdale had just completed a translation of the Bible, which now made its way to England. Another colleague of Tyndale's, John Rogers (who took the pen name Thomas Matthew) also completed an English Bible (1537) that received royal sanction. Not completely happy with either, Thomas Cromwell, vicar-general under Henry VIII, commissioned Miles Coverdale to do a thorough revision of the Bible based upon the Matthew Bible. This version was known as the "Great Bible" because of its size. Unfortunately, toward the end of his reign, Henry condemned the Tyndale and Coverdale versions in a 1543 Act of Parliament.

◀ A portrait of Henry VIII

▲ **TITLE PAGE OF THE GREAT BIBLE** This was the first "Authorized Version" before the translation of its better known 1611 counterpart.

◄ **MILES COVERDALE (1488–1569)** Coverdale was an Augustinian friar who became enthusiastic for the reformation of the church. He undertook two translations of the Bible: the Coverdale Bible and the Great Bible.

THOMAS CROMWELL (1485–1540) Cromwell was the chief advisor to Henry VIII. Sympathetic to the Reformation principles, he commissioned the translation of the Great Bible. He also issued injunctions ordering a Bible to be provided in every church.

TITLE PAGE TO THE 1535 COVERDALE BIBLE

This translation was based largely on Tyndale's version and influenced by the German versions.

◄ **A MATTHEW'S BIBLE OPENED TO THE GOSPEL OF JOHN** This version brought to completion a translation of the Old Testament that Tyndale had been unable to complete.

JOHN CALVIN AND THE GENEVA BIBLE (1560)

▲ Introductory page of a first edition (1560) Geneva Bible.

When Mary Queen of Scots became the British monarch in 1553, people sympathetic to the English Reformation found themselves the objects of persecution. Many fled England to various places on the continent where they could escape Mary's repressive measures. One key Protestant center was Geneva, Switzerland, where John Calvin (1509–1564) was active. One of these English refugees was William Whittingham, a brother-in-law to Calvin as well as an Oxford scholar and successor to John Knox as pastor to the English congregation in Geneva. Whittingham undertook a revision of the English Bible that he brought to completion in 1560. This new version, based principally upon the Matthew's Bible, came to be known as the Geneva Bible after the city where it was produced. The Geneva Bible had extensive marginal notes that tended to reflect Calvinistic interpretations of Scripture as well as occasional anti-Roman sentiments. Mary Queen of Scots died two years before the Bible was finished and her sucessor, Elizabeth I, was much more sympathetic to English Protestantism, which paved the way for a friendly reception of the Bible in England. The Geneva Bible became very popular for private use in England. It was the Bible used by William Shakespeare, John Bunyan, and the Puritans.

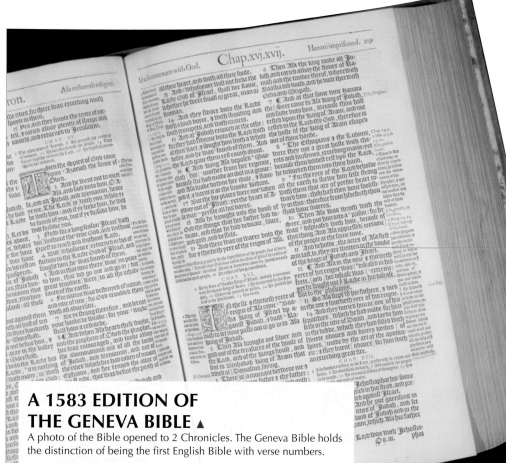

A 1583 EDITION OF THE GENEVA BIBLE ▲

A photo of the Bible opened to 2 Chronicles. The Geneva Bible holds the distinction of being the first English Bible with verse numbers.

▲ A PORTRAIT OF JOHN CALVIN IN HIS STUDY Although Calvin was not directly involved in the translation, his influence is seen throughout the Bible in the study notes.

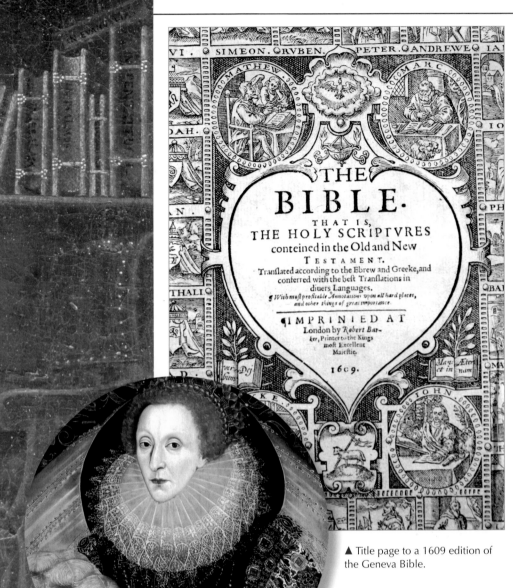

▲ Title page to a 1609 edition of the Geneva Bible.

▼ **QUEEN ELIZABETH I** was the daughter of Henry VIII and Anne Boleyn. Whittingham dedicated the Bible to the Queen.

▶ **TABLE OF CONTENTS FROM A 1609 EDITION OF THE GENEVA BIBLE** This Bible included the Apocryphal books.

◀ **THE GOSPEL OF JOHN IN A 1609 EDITION OF THE GENEVA BIBLE** The Bible features verse divisions, chapter summaries, and extensive study notes.

Mount Olivet is .2. mile from Ieru
salem east and by south. Gethsemani
a village lieth at the foote of the
mount. betwixt the same and Ieru-
salē. Bethphage a village lieth nor
farre from it. Also in the vale, be-
twixte the mount aud Ierusalem,
Golgatha or the mount Caluarie lieth, hard by Ierusalem, vveast and
by north.

▲ A map of the land of Israel in the Bishop's Bible (1568).

STUDY BIBLES

Although study Bibles may seem like a fairly recent innovation, their roots go back hundreds of years. The features that characterize contemporary study Bibles, such as cross-references, footnotes with historical and theological information, maps, illustrations, and introductions to books, can be seen in early English versions as well as in the Luther Bible. A cursory examination of some of these ancient Bibles makes them appear as not too different from their contemporary cousins.

► The Luther Bible (1534) makes use of chapter summaries, cross references, and marginal notations. This is the first few verses of Isaiah 53.

▼ THE GENEVA BIBLE (1560) contains concise chapter summaries and extensive verse-by-verse notes that explain difficult concepts, give historical information, and provide some doctrinal reflection. The footnotes for Isaiah 53 explain how the passage is fulfilled in Christ.

should bee wrought, whereof this was a figure.
man, Christ in his person was not esteemed. p He shal spread his word through many nations. q In signe of reverence, and as being astonished at his excellency.
r By the preaching of the Gospel.

CHAP. LIII.

1 *Of Christ and his kingdome, whose word fewe will beleeue.* 6 *All men are sinners.* 11 *Christ is our righteousnesse,* 12 *and is dead for our sinne.*

a The Prophet sheweth that very few shall receiue this their preaching of Christ, and of their deliverance by him, Iohn 12.38. rom. 10.16.
b Meaning that none can beleeue but whose hearts God toucheth with the vertue of his holy Spirit.

WHo a wil beleeue our report? & to whom is the b arme of the Lord reueiled?

2 But hee shall growe vp before him as a branch, and as a c roote out of a dry d ground: he hath neither forme nor beauty: when we shall see him, there shall be no forme that we should desire him.

3 He is despised and reiected of men: he is a man full of sorrowes, and hath experience of e infirmities: we hid as it were our faces from him, he was despised, and we esteemed him not.

c The beginning of Christs kingdome shalbe small and contemptible in the sight of man, but it shall growe wonderfully, and flourish before God. d Reade Chap. 11.1. e Which was by Gods singular providence for the comfort of sinners, Hebr 4.15.

hath moe children the
the Lord.

2 c Enlarge the p
them spread out the cu
spare not: stretch out t
stakes.

3 For thou shalt
and on the left, and th
tiles, and dwell in the

4 Feare not: for
neither shalt thou be e
not bee put to shame
shame of thy d youth,
reproch of thy e wido

5 For hee that f n
(whose name is the Lo
deemer the holy One
her. Her deliuerance vnder
complished, when the came t
for the great number of chil
roome to lodge them. d
e When as thou wast refu
thee by his holy Spirit.

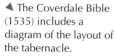

◄ The Coverdale Bible (1535) includes a diagram of the layout of the tabernacle.

ℭThe Epistle of
the Apostle. S. Paul vnto the Ephesians.

ℭThe first Chapter.

ℭThe euerlasting ordinaunce and election God in saving all men through Christ Iesus sonne: we are ordeined vnto good workes, the minion of Christ.

Rom. i. a:
i. Cor. i. a
ii. Cor. i. a
i. Pet. i. a
Gala i. a:
i. Pet. i. a

Paul an Apostle of Ie Christ by the wil of g To the Sainctes, wh are at Ephesus and the which beleue on sus Christ. * Grac with you and peace f God our father, and from the Lord J Christ. * Blessed be god the father of Lord Iesus Christ, which hath blesse with all maner of spirituall blessin heauenly things by Christ, accordin

▶ The Great Bible (1539), produced by Miles Coverdale, includes chapter summaries and cross references. Notice how there are no verse divisions. This is the beginning of Paul's letter to the Ephesians.

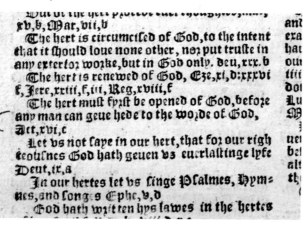

xv. b, Mar, vii, b

ℭThe hert is circumcised of God, to the intent that it should loue none other, nor put truste in any exterior worke, but in God only. deu, xxx. b

ℭThe hert is renewed of God, Eze, xi, d; xxxvi f, Iere, xxiii, f, iii, Reg, xviii, f

ℭThe hert must first be opened of God, before any man can geue hede to the worde of God, Act, xvi, c

Let vs not saye in our hert, that for our righteousnes God hath geuen vs euerlastinge lyfe Deut, ix, a

In our hertes let vs singe Psalmes, Hymnes, and songs Ephe, v, d

God hath writ ten hys lawes in the hertes

◄ THE INTRODUCTORY PAGES OF MATTHEW'S BIBLE (1537) includes an alphabetical listing of topics under which are a variety of precepts with relevant Scriptural references. These are a few of the listings under "heart."

The notes.

a. He dwelleth wyth his wyfe accordinge to knowledge, that taketh her as a necessarye healper, and not as a bonde seruaunte or a bonde slaue. And yf she be not obedient and healpfull vnto hym, endeuoureth to beate the feare of God into her heade, that therby she maye be compelled to learne her duitie and do it. But chiefely he muste be ware that he halte not in anye parte of his duitie to her ward. For his euill exemple, shall destroye more then al the instruccios he can geue, shall edifie.
b. Erasmus in his annotacions, noteth out of Saint Ierome, that this honoure is not the honoure wyth the knees, nother the decking

▼ Matthew's Bible (1537), produced by John Rogers, has extensive explanatory notes at the end of chapters. This controversial applicational note to 1 Peter 3:7 garnered it the nickname "the Wife-Beater's Bible."

¶ A Table to make plaine the difficultie that [is] found in S. Matthew and S. Luke, touching the generation [of] Iesus Christ the sonne of Dauid, and his right successour in the kingdome : which discription begin-neth at Dauid, and no higher, bicause the difficultie is only in his posteritie.

Saint Mathewe.	Dauid begate	Saint Luke.
Solomon king.		Nathan the kings
Roboam.	The posteritie of So-	brother.
Abia.	lomon left in Ochosi-	Mathatha.
Asa.	as, whereby the kyng-	Menna.
Iosaphat.	dome was transported	Melcha.
Ioram.	to the line of Nathan,	Eliacim.
Ochosias.	in the person of Ioas	Iona.
	son to Iuda.	Ioseph.
		Iuda. *

Or better vnderstanding of the [...] this Table, ye shall note, that th[...] listes S. Matthew and S. Luk[...] uersly resited the generation of [...] our Christe, accoding to the fle[...] tend both to one end : that is, to [...] accoding to that which is w[...] ended of the royal bloude [...] the kingdom. So the [...] s: that S. Matthew [...] from father to sonn[...]

▲ The Bishops' Bible contains many study aids, such as this table helping the reader to understand the geneaologies in Matthew and Luke.

◄ Isaiah 53:1–3 in a 1575 edition of the Bishops' Bible.

▼ Matthew Parker (1504–1575) was the Archbishop of Canterbury who commissioned the Bishops' Bible.

THE PREDECESSOR TO THE KING JAMES VERSION: THE BISHOPS' BIBLE (1568)

The days of official suppression of Bible reading had passed and the English people enjoyed the opportunity to freely read and study the Bible. During the mid–1560s, under the reign of Queen Elizabeth I, the Geneva Bible was far more popular among the people than the authorized version commissioned by Henry VIII (the Great Bible). This was troubling to church and state officials because of the political nature of some of the notes in the margins of the Geneva Bible. In an effort to remedy the situation, the Archbishop of Canterbury, Matthew Parker, put together a team of church bishops to produce a new authorized version. This new translation, based upon the Great Bible of 1539, was completed in 1568 and became known as "the Bishops' Bible" because of the number of bishops who participated in the project. This second "authorized version" superseded the Great Bible in popularity but was never able to supplant the appeal of the Geneva Bible.

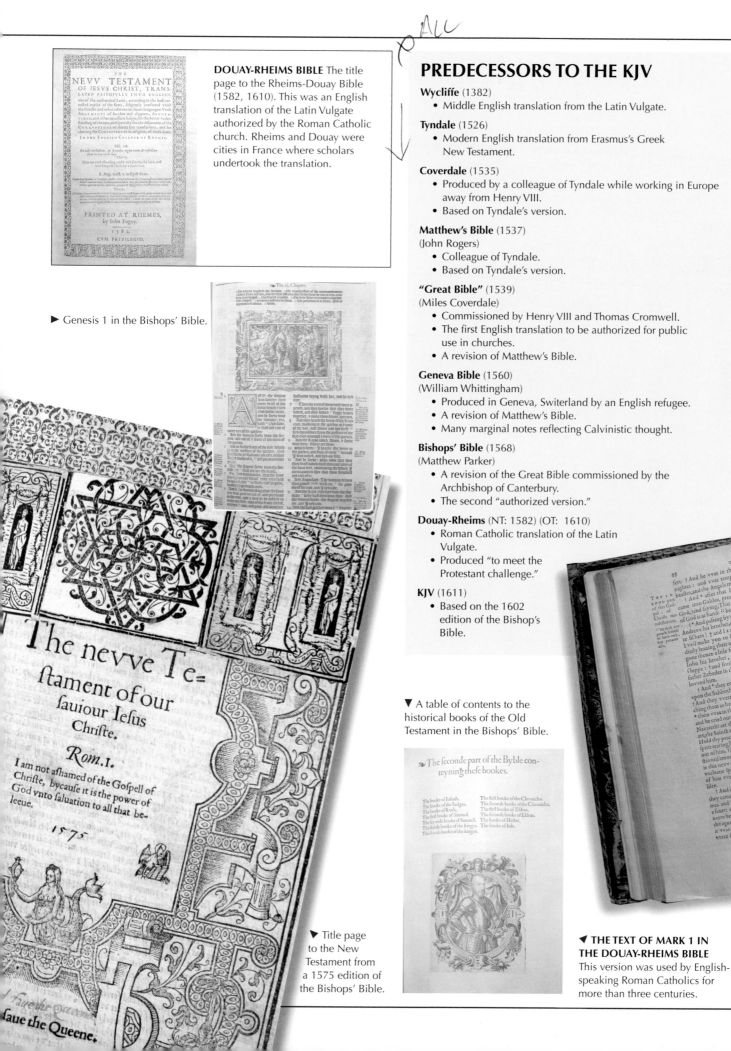

DOUAY-RHEIMS BIBLE The title page to the Rheims-Douay Bible (1582, 1610). This was an English translation of the Latin Vulgate authorized by the Roman Catholic church. Rheims and Douay were cities in France where scholars undertook the translation.

► Genesis 1 in the Bishops' Bible.

PREDECESSORS TO THE KJV

Wycliffe (1382)
• Middle English translation from the Latin Vulgate.

Tyndale (1526)
• Modern English translation from Erasmus's Greek New Testament.

Coverdale (1535)
• Produced by a colleague of Tyndale while working in Europe away from Henry VIII.
• Based on Tyndale's version.

Matthew's Bible (1537)
(John Rogers)
• Colleague of Tyndale.
• Based on Tyndale's version.

"Great Bible" (1539)
(Miles Coverdale)
• Commissioned by Henry VIII and Thomas Cromwell.
• The first English translation to be authorized for public use in churches.
• A revision of Matthew's Bible.

Geneva Bible (1560)
(William Whittingham)
• Produced in Geneva, Switerland by an English refugee.
• A revision of Matthew's Bible.
• Many marginal notes reflecting Calvinistic thought.

Bishops' Bible (1568)
(Matthew Parker)
• A revision of the Great Bible commissioned by the Archbishop of Canterbury.
• The second "authorized version."

Douay-Rheims (NT: 1582) (OT: 1610)
• Roman Catholic translation of the Latin Vulgate.
• Produced "to meet the Protestant challenge."

KJV (1611)
• Based on the 1602 edition of the Bishop's Bible.

▼ A table of contents to the historical books of the Old Testament in the Bishops' Bible.

▼ Title page to the New Testament from a 1575 edition of the Bishops' Bible.

◄ **THE TEXT OF MARK 1 IN THE DOUAY-RHEIMS BIBLE**
This version was used by English-speaking Roman Catholics for more than three centuries.

THE KING JAMES VERSION OF 1611

Although King James VI of Scotland had for thirty-six years ruled a country where Puritanism and Presbyterianism flourished, he detested the Geneva Bible. His hostility to the translation stemmed mainly from a handful of marginal notes that he saw as opposed to his firm conviction about the "divine right of kings"—a belief that kings are ordained by God and endowed with divine authority for their work on earth. When he succeeded Elizabeth and became king of England in 1603 (and then known as James I), he convened a conference at Hampton Court to handle the problem of religious division in the country. The most significant outcome of this conference was the resolution to revise the English Bible. Over fifty scholars were appointed to the task. They were instructed to use the 1602 edition of the Bishops' Bible as the basis and that it should be "as little altered as the truth of the original will permit." Their diligent labor resulted in a translation that made the clearest, most eloquent use of the English language yet. The King James Bible of 1611, as it came to be called, endeared itself to the hearts of many generations of English speaking people throughout the world. The King James Version of the Bible we use today, called "the Oxford standard edition," actually differs significantly from the original of 1611. It is based on a 1769 revision that followed several earlier revisions carried out in the 150 years between 1611 and 1769. Not only has the King James Version been the most popular Bible in history, it has also been the most influential book in the history of the English language.

◀ **KING JAMES I OF ENGLAND AND VI OF SCOTLAND (1566–1625)** He firmly believed that monarchy is God's chosen form of government and that rebellion against a monarch is always sin. His annoyance at the Geneva Bible, which seemed to contradict this in certain notes, helped catalyze his support for a new version.

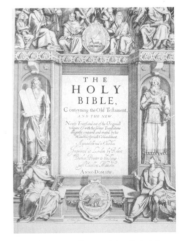

▲ Title page of an original 1611 edition of the King James Bible.

◄ AN ILLUSTRATION OF THE FAMILY TREE of Adam and Eve in an original edition of the King James Bible. The Bible also contained about nine thousand marginal references but no study notes.

SOME ARCHAIC EXPRESSIONS FROM THE KING JAMES VERSION (OXFORD STANDARD EDITION)

The expressions illustrate how language changes and becomes difficult to understand for succeeding generations. One warrant for Bible translations is to update the language.

"sick of the palsy" (Mk 2:3)

"thou hast possessed my reins" (Ps 139:13)

"decayeth and waxeth old" (Heb 8:13)

"not in chambering and wantonness" (Rom 13:13)

"the instruments also of the churl are evil" (Isa 32:7)

"sit at meat with thee" (Luke 14:10)

"Isaac was sporting with his wife" (Gen 26:8)

"by his neesings a light doth shine" (Job 41:18)

"ye have respect to him that weareth the gay clothing" (James 2:3)

"but when divers were hardened, and believed not" (Acts 19:9)

▼ The King James Bible contains the so-called *Comma Johanneum*: "the Father, the Word, and the Holy Ghost: and these three are one. And there are three that bear witness in earth" (1 John 5:7–8). Although the reading appears in the Latin Vulgate, it is not found in any Greek manuscript prior to 1520.

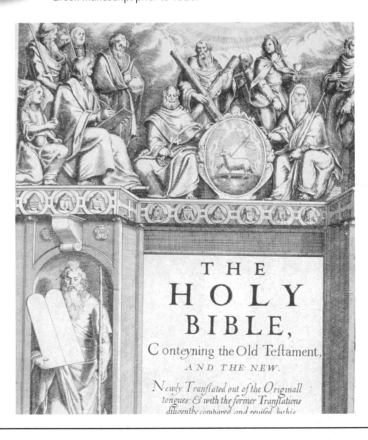

◄ THE TEXT OF THE TEN COMMANDMENTS (EXODUS 20) IN A 1611 EDITION OF THE KING JAMES BIBLE In an unfortunate printer's error in the 1631 edition, the word "not" was accidentally omitted from "thou shalt not commit adultery." This edition came to be known as the "Wicked Bible."

◄ The original King James version included the Apocrypha. It was not omitted until 1826.

◀ After Wycliffe's death by natural causes, his remains were exhumed, burned, and thrown into a nearby stream. Nicholas of Hereford and John Purvey, colleagues of Wycliffe, were jailed and forced to recant. Others had Bibles tied around their necks and were burned at the stake.

A FORBIDDEN BOOK WORTH DYING FOR

Although loved and cherished, the Bible has also been feared, hated, and forbidden. How could it be otherwise? It is difficult to be neutral and dispassionate about a book that claims to be inspired by God with a message of life and death significance. Throughout history there have been people who have done their best to suppress the Bible and its message by burning it, outlawing it, and threatening people who read it. Yet there have also been plenty who have committed their lives completely to this book and engaged in every manner of sacrifice to make it available and further its message. Numerous Bibles were destroyed as early as the fourth century when the Roman emperor Diocletian ordered churches to be razed to the ground and the Scriptures to be burned. After the invention of printing, many Christian leaders sacrificed their lives to make the Bible available to people in their own language. And countless people faced horrible persecution under Communism for owning and reading Bibles. Such persecution is not a thing of the past. The Bible is still forbidden in many places. People continue to risk their lives to get the Bible to those who do not have it, and people still die for reading it.

► Cuthbert Tunstall, bishop of London during the time of Tyndale, oversaw the burning of confiscated Tyndale Bibles in London. Tunstall called Tyndale's Bible a "pestiferous and most pernicious poison."

◄ People sympathetic to Tyndale's vision for making the English Bible available in England helped smuggle the Bible into the country in cotton bales and in other containers.

◄ **BIBLE BURNING?** Sometimes fellow Christians claim to find reason for burning the Bible. This metal box is filled with the ashes of a Revised Standard Version of the Bible. A pastor burned it with a blowtorch shortly after it was published protesting that is was "a heretical, communist-inspired Bible."

◄ The Roman Emperor Diocletian, who reigned from 284–305, unleashed a horrible period of persecution against Christians that resulted in the burning of many Bibles.

◄ **BROTHER ANDREW** When he traveled to Poland in 1955, he discovered an underground church that did not have Bibles. The young Dutch missionary smuggled a suitcase full of Bibles to them and began a worldwide ministry of getting Bibles to persecuted peoples.

QUEEN MARY I (MARY TUDOR)

She reigned over England from 1553 to 1568. She opposed the Protestant Reformation in England and burned at the stake some of those involved in making English translations of the Bible, including John Rogers and Thomas Cranmer.

THE FIRST BIBLE PRINTED IN AMERICA: THE ALGONQUIN BIBLE (1663)

The first Bible ever to be printed in the New World was not in English, French, or German, but in Algonquin. It was the translation of both Old and New Testaments into the language of a Native American tribe by an Englishman named John Eliot (1604–1690). Eliot was a Puritan who was educated at Cambridge and emigrated to the New World in 1631. He arrived at the Massachusetts Bay Company on the same boat as the family of John Winthrop, the first governor of the Colony. One of the express goals of the Colony was to reach out and serve the spiritual needs of the Native Americans. In fact, the Massachusetts general court ordered that, "efforts to promote the diffusion of Christianity among aboriginal inhabitants be made with all diligence." Eliot became the teaching pastor of the church in Roxbury, where he served for fifty-seven years. With the support of his congregation, he began evangelizing the Indians and learning their language. By 1674 there were 4,000 converts among fourteen different villages. The "Apostle to the Indians" completed his translation of the New Testament in 1661 and the Old Testament in 1663.

▼ **THE SEAL OF THE MASSACHUSETTS BAY COLONY** It depicts an Indian saying, "Come over and help us," an allusion to Acts 16:9, Paul's Macedonian vision.

THE TITLE PAGE OF THE ALGONQUIN BIBLE (1663)

This volume stands as a tribute to many of the early colonists who exhibited selfless love and a passionate care for the native Americans.

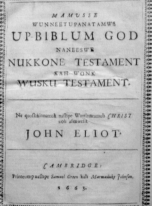

► **JOHN ELIOT** This diligent pastor, missionary, and translator used to say, "Prayer and pains through faith in Christ Jesus will accomplish anything."

◄ A sixteenth-century painting of an Algonquin Indian.

◄ An opened Algonquin Bible

◄ **THE LANDING OF GOVERNOR JOHN WINTHROP AT SALEM, MASSACHUSETTS, IN 1630** These colonists came to the New World during the reign of Charles I of England (1625–1649), the son of King James I (1603–1625), whose name is forever connected to the Authorized Version of 1611.

require special notice; first, the Greek Text which it appears to have represented, and secondly, the character of the Translation itself.

1. With regard to the Greek Text, it would appear that, if to some extent the Translators exercised an independent judgement, it was mainly in choosing amongst readings contained in the principal editions of the Greek Text that had appeared in the sixteenth century. Wherever they seem to have followed a reading which is not found in any of those editions, their rendering may probably be traced to the Latin Vulgate. Their chief guides appear to have been the later editions of Stephanus and of Beza, and also, to a certain extent, the Complutensian Polyglott. All these were founded for the most part on manuscripts of late date, few in number, and used with little critical skill. But in those days it could hardly have been otherwise. Nearly all the more ancient of the documentary authorities have become known only within the last two centuries; some of the most important of them, indeed, within the last few years. Their publication has called forth not only improved editions of the Greek Text, but a succession of instructive discussions on the variations which have been brought to light, and on the best modes of distinguishing original readings from changes introduced in the course of transcription. While therefore it has long been the opinion of all scholars that the commonly received text needed thorough revision, it is but recently that materials have been acquired for executing such a work with even approximate completeness.

2. The character of the Translation itself will be best estimated by considering the leading rules under which it was made, and the extent to which these rules

A MONUMENTAL REVISION OF THE KING JAMES VERSION:
THE ENGLISH REVISED VERSION AND THE AMERICAN STANDARD VERSION

Whereas only nine years passed after the publication of the Bishops' Bible and its revision in the King James Bible of 1611, over 250 years passed before the church decided to make a through revision of the King James version. Part of the reason for this can be attributed to the superb job done by the translators of the KJV. By the mid–1800s, however, scholars began recognizing the need to update the King James Bible on the basis of a far better collection of Greek manuscripts than had been previously available. The King James Bible had ultimately been based on only a half dozen late medieval manuscripts. But now there were numerous Greek manuscripts available, including the two ancient parchment manuscripts known as Sinaiticus and Vaticanus. In 1870, a British church commission authorized a complete revision to be made of the KJV. The New Testament was brought to completion in 1881 and the entire Bible was finished in 1885. An American edition of this revision was published in 1901 and called the American Standard Version. The English Revised Version was not as well received as the translators had hoped. Charles Spurgeon summed it up well when he quipped that the new version was "strong in Greek, weak in English." The American counterpart was well received, but neither version supplanted the popularity of the King James Version.

▶ Philip Schaff, well known for his multi-volume *History of the Christian Church*, was the chair of the American committee responsible for the American Standard Version.

A PAGE FROM AN 1869 EDITION OF TISCHENDORF'S GREEK NEW TESTAMENT

This volume as well as Greek texts edited by Samuel Tregelles and Westcott and Hort were used by translators in the preparation of the new versions. Notice how the presence of "in Ephesus" is now questioned in Ephesians 1:1 by placing it in brackets.

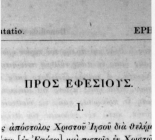

▲ The American Standard Version of 1901

◀ **THE ASV TEXT OF ISAIAH 52–53** The ASV included subject headings and cross-references.

▼ **FOOTNOTE ON THE LONGER ENDING OF MARK FROM THE ENGLISH REVISED VERSION** The "two oldest Greek manuscripts" refers to codices Sinaiticus and Vaticanus.

lieved they them.

14 And afterward ᶜ he was manifested ᵈ unto the eleven themselves as they sat at meat; and he ᵉ upbraided them with their ᶠ unbelief and ᵍ hardness of heart, because ʰ they believed not them which had seen him after he was risen. 15 And he said unto them, ⁱ Go ye into all the world, and ʲ preach the gospel to ʲ ᵏ the whole

1 The two oldest Greek manuscripts, and some other authorities, omit from ver. 9 to the end. Some other authorities have a different ending to the Gospel.
2 Gr. *demons.*

4 ᵍ Mt. 27 60.   24 10.   v Jn. 16 20.   w Lk. 6 25,
5 ʰ *Cp.* Lk. 24 4, Jn. 20 11, 12.   Ja. 4 9, Rev. 18 11, 15, 19.
ⁱ 2 Mac. 3 26.   ʲ *Cp.* ch. 9 3, Dn. 7 9,   11 x Lk. 24 11; *see* ver. 16.
Jn. 20 12, Ac. 1 10.   ᵏ Rev. 6 11, 7 9;   12 y ver. 14, Jn. 21 1, 14.   z Lk. 9

◀ **THE WESTCOTT–HORT GREEK NEW TESTAMENT** This modern critical edition was prepared by two scholars who worked on the ERV.

▶ The famous New Testament scholar, J. B. Lightfoot, was a member of the translation committee for the English Revised Version. Other committee members included B. F. Westcott, F. J.

SUCCESSORS TO THE ASV: THE MODERN VERSIONS

The American Standard Version served churches in the United States well for a generation, but its greater contribution was its role as the forerunner to a new era of Bible translations. Versions such as the Revised Standard Version, the New American Standard Bible, the New International Version, as well as most other contemporary translations are deeply indebted to the ASV. The first revision of the ASV was published in 1952 as the Revised Standard Version. It made significant improvements on the overly literal ASV. Translators also took into account the more recent manuscript discoveries including the early papyri discovered in Egypt. The beauty and dignity of the English used in this revision endeared itself to both American and British readers. In 1971, the Lockman Foundation commissioned its own revision of the ASV and published the New American Standard Bible. The translation was carried out by an interdenominational group of evangelical scholars. They employed a more word-for-word translation approach than the translators of the RSV, which resulted in a version that reflected a translation philosophy similar to the ASV. The translation that has emerged, however, as the most popular (especially among evangelicals) is the New International Version. It is a completely new translation of the Greek and Hebrew that tries to combine readability with fidelity to the form of the original text.

◄ **PROFESSOR BRUCE METZGER, EMERITUS PROFESSOR AT PRINCETON THEOLOGICAL SEMINARY** Professor Metzger was one of the editors of the standard Greek text used by scholars and translators around the world. He also served as an editor of both the Revised Standard Version and the New Revised Standard Version.

◄ **NEW INTERNATIONAL VERSION (1978)** The NIV has been the most popular version of this generation, with more than 215 million copies sold or distributed worldwide.

► **TODAYS NEW INTERNATIONAL VERSION (2005)** Nearly thirty years after the publication of the NIV, the Committee for Bible Translation has offered a revision. The translators have sought to offer an updated English translation (including gender accurate langauge) as well as to take into account thousands of suggestions for improvement they had collected over the years.

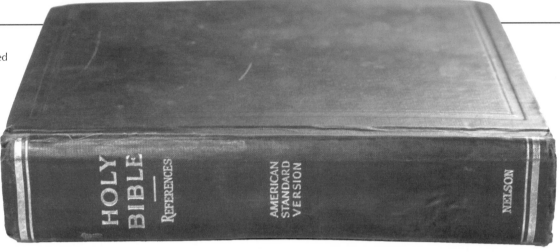

► **AMERICAN STANDARD VERSION (1901)** Many viewed this version as excessively literal and somewhat difficult to read. Nevertheless, it served churches well for nearly two generations although it never gained the popularity of the KJV.

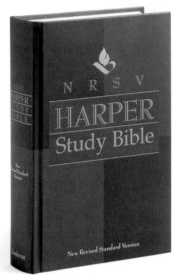

► **NEW AMERICAN STANDARD (1971)** After its publication, the NASB became very popular among evangelicals, selling millions of copies. Its popularity was eclipsed less than a decade later by the publication of the NIV.

◄ **NEW REVISED STANDARD VERSION (1990)** This revision took into account new textual insights from the Dead Sea Scrolls and Greek papyri, updated archaic expressions, and eliminated masculine-oriented language.

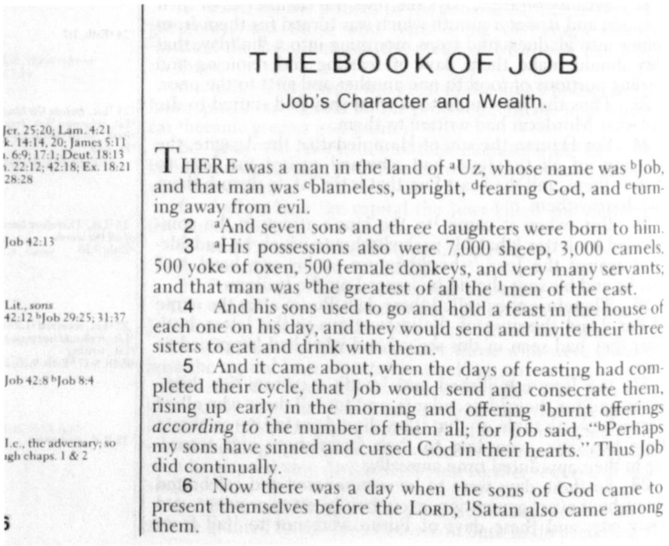

THE BOOK OF JOB

Job's Character and Wealth.

THERE was a man in the land of ᵃUz, whose name was ᵇJob, and that man was ᶜblameless, upright, ᵈfearing God, and ᵉturning away from evil.

2 ᵃAnd seven sons and three daughters were born to him.

3 ᵃHis possessions also were 7,000 sheep, 3,000 camels, 500 yoke of oxen, 500 female donkeys, and very many servants; and that man was ᵇthe greatest of all the ¹men of the east.

4 And his sons used to go and hold a feast in the house of each one on his day, and they would send and invite their three sisters to eat and drink with them.

5 And it came about, when the days of feasting had completed their cycle, that Job would send and consecrate them, rising up early in the morning and offering ᵃburnt offerings *according to* the number of them all; for Job said, "ᵇPerhaps my sons have sinned and cursed God in their hearts." Thus Job did continually.

6 Now there was a day when the sons of God came to present themselves before the LORD, ¹Satan also came among them.

Reference notes (left margin of Job page):
Jer. 25:20; Lam. 4:21
k. 14:14, 20; James 5:11
. 6:9; 17:1; Deut. 18:13
. 22:12; 42:18; Ex. 21:28:28

Job 42:13

Lit., sons
42:12 ᵇJob 29:25; 31:37

Job 42:8 ᵇJob 8:4

I.e., the adversary; so
gh chaps. 1 & 2

SUCCESSORS TO THE ASV

English Revised Version (1881)
Authorized revision of the King James Version

American Standard Version (1901)
Authorized revision of the King James Version

Revised Standard Version (1952)
Revision of the American Standard Version

New American Standard Bible (1971)
Evangelical revision of the American Standard Version

New Revised Standard Version (1990)
Revision of the Revised Standard Version

New International Version (1978)
Independent translation by Evangelicals, but using a similar textual basis to the ASV

New American Standard Bible (1995 Update)
Revision of the New American Standard Bible

¹⁹Mm 3985.   Cp 5...
⁷Mm 1598.   ⁸Mm 2824...

ALL ANCIENT MANUSCRIPTS IN ONE VOLUME

BIBLIA HEBRAICA STUTTGARTENSIA AND THE UNITED BIBLE SOCIETY'S GREEK TEXT

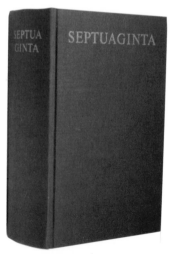

▲ THE GREEK OLD TESTAMENT, KNOWN AS THE SEPTUAGINT
This critical edition also contains notes with the relevant manuscript information.

It is now no longer necessary for Bible translators to travel to libraries all over the world to consult individual manuscripts. Scholars have created a way to make the relevant manuscript information available in one volume through the modern critical editions of the Hebrew Bible and the Greek New Testament. These volumes contain extensive footnotes, called a "critical apparatus," at the bottom of every page. The notes not only record instances of manuscript variation on the wording of the text, but they employ an extensive system of symbols and abbreviations to indicate precisely which manuscripts contain one reading and which contain another. The editors of these texts have attempted to reconstruct the original text not on the basis of a handful of manuscripts or one or two favorites, but on the entire manuscript tradition. The end result is an extraordinarily accurate edition of both the Old Testament and the New Testament in the original languages. These critical editions stand behind virtually all modern translations of the Bible and are used regularly by Bible teachers, seminary professors, pastors, and laypeople who have learned Greek and Hebrew. Both editions are published by the United Bible Societies.

◀ THE GREEK NEW TESTAMENT

Whereas prior to the time of Luther, Calvin, and the Reformers, no pastors knew Greek and Hebrew, now most seminaries *require* pastoral students to gain some level of proficiency in the original languages of the Scripture.

▶ The Greek New Testament opened to Ephesians 1.

◀ The bottom of this sample page from the Hebrew Bible (*Biblia Hebraica Stuttgartensia*) displays three lines of Hebrew text from Isaiah 53:8–9 and two levels of footnotes. The first level, in small print, makes reference to Masoretic notes. The second level indicates manuscript variation.

WHAT THE NOTES INDICATE

The superscript numeral '2' indicates that scribes have written "in Ephesus" into the margins of Codex Sinaiticus (א) and Codex Vaticanus (B).

The symbol Byz indicates that "in Ephesus" is in several thousand minuscule manuscripts from the 10th to the 15th centuries.

The symbols following "in Ephesus" indicate manuscripts that contain the phrase.

These symbols indicate that "in Ephesus" is in a variety of ancient versions, including the Old Latin (it), the Vulgate, Syriac, Coptic, Armenian, Ethiopic, Georgian, and Slavonic.

The symbols following "omit" indicate manuscripts that do not contain the phrase.

The first three symbols indicate that an early papyrus, Codex Sinaiticus (א), and Codex Vaticanus (B) all do not have "in Ephesus."

◀ THE HEBREW BIBLE

This is the Hebrew Bible currently used by biblical scholars and translators. This modern critical edition was first published in 1967. At left is the Hebrew Bible opened to the text of Isaiah 52 and 53. Its predecessor was prepared about forty years earlier by Rudolph Kittel. The Hebrew text is based upon the eleventh-century codex Leningradensis. Any variations from this manuscript in other Hebrew manuscripts, the Dead Sea Scrolls, and the Septuagint are noted in the footnotes (the critical apparatus).

EARLY PARALLEL BIBLES

The oldest known parallel Bible can be traced back as early as the third century AD, when the famous church father Origen (AD 185–254) created a six-column volume of the Old Testament. The columns contained the Hebrew text, a Greek transliteration of the Hebrew, and four different Greek translations of the Hebrew Bible. Unfortunately, no copy of this monumental and enormous work has survived. The earliest parallel Bible that has survived can be traced back to the fifth century AD, when a scribe created a "bilingual" Greek and Latin manuscript of the New Testament. Such a volume would have been an immense help to a reader who was a native Latin speaker but wanted to cross-check the Latin translation with the original text. Shortly after the invention of printing, a Spanish cardinal by the name of Francisco Ximenes de Cisneros organized the preparation of a parallel Bible in Alcalá, Spain (called Complutum in Latin). This expensive four-volume set included the Hebrew, Aramaic (Targums), Greek, and Latin texts set out in parallel columns and was completed in stages between 1514 and 1522. Since then, numerous forms and configurations of parallel Bibles have been created and used in the church. Parallel Bibles displaying versions of different languages are known as "polyglots" (many tongues).

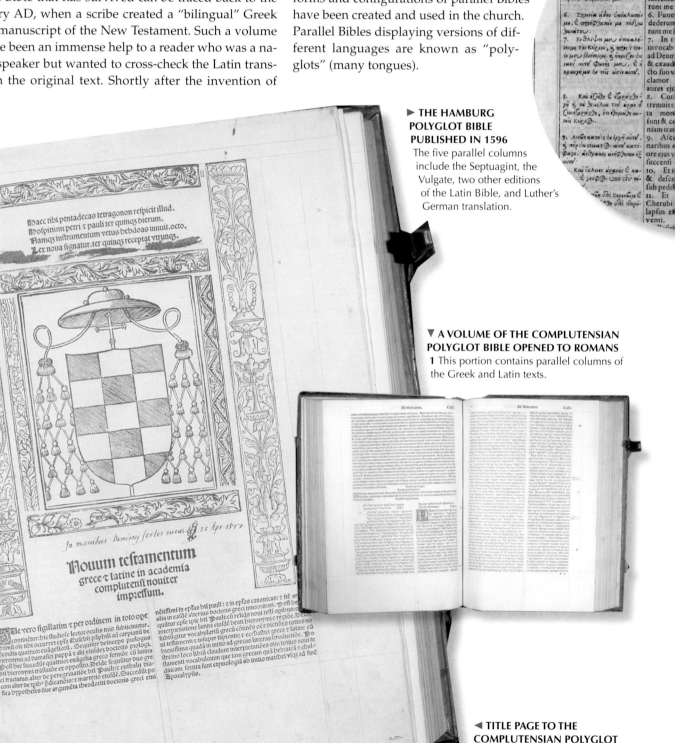

▶ **THE HAMBURG POLYGLOT BIBLE PUBLISHED IN 1596** The five parallel columns include the Septuagint, the Vulgate, two other editions of the Latin Bible, and Luther's German translation.

▼ **A VOLUME OF THE COMPLUTENSIAN POLYGLOT BIBLE OPENED TO ROMANS** **1** This portion contains parallel columns of the Greek and Latin texts.

◀ **TITLE PAGE TO THE COMPLUTENSIAN POLYGLOT BIBLE** Only 600 copies of this Bible were published.

ΕΥΑΓΓΕΛΙΟΝ
ΚΑΤΑ ΙΩΑΝΝΗΝ.

I.

Verbum dei caro factum. Iohannis baptistae de Christo testimonia. De vocatione Andreae et socii, item Petri, Philippi et Nathanahelis.

1 (1.3) Ἐν ἀρχῇ ἦν ὁ λόγος, καὶ ὁ λόγος ἦν πρὸς τὸν θεόν, καὶ θεὸς ἦν ὁ λόγος. 2 οὗτος ἦν ἐν ἀρχῇ πρὸς τὸν θεόν. 3 πάντα δι᾽ αὐτοῦ ἐγένετο, καὶ χωρὶς αὐτοῦ ἐγένετο οὐδὲ ἓν ὃ γέγονεν. 4 ἐν αὐτῷ ζωὴ ἦν, καὶ ἡ ζωὴ ἦν τὸ φῶς τῶν ἀνθρώπων· 5 καὶ τὸ φῶς ἐν τῇ σκοτίᾳ φαίνει, καὶ ἡ σκοτία αὐτὸ οὐ κατέλαβεν. 6 (2.3) Ἐγένετο ἄνθρωπος, ἀπεσταλμένος παρὰ θεοῦ, ὄνομα αὐτῷ Ἰωάννης· 7 οὗτος ἦλθεν εἰς μαρτυρίαν, ἵνα μαρτυρήσῃ περὶ τοῦ φωτός, ἵνα πάντες πιστεύσωσιν δι᾽ αὐτοῦ. 8 οὐκ ἦν ἐκεῖνος τὸ φῶς, ἀλλ᾽ ἵνα μαρτυρήσῃ περὶ τοῦ φωτός. 9 (3.3) Ἦν τὸ φῶς τὸ ἀληθινόν, ὃ φωτίζει πάντα ἄνθρωπον, ἐρχόμενον εἰς τὸν κόσμον. 10 ἐν τῷ κόσμῳ ἦν, καὶ

EVANGELIUM
SECUNDUM IOHANNEM.

I.

Verbum dei caro factum. Iohannis baptistae de Christo testimonia. De vocatione Andreae et socii, item Petri, Philippi et Nathanahelis.

1 (1.3) In principio erat verbum, et verbum erat apud deum, et deus erat verbum. 2 Hoc erat in principio apud deum. 3 Omnia per ipsum facta sunt, et sine ipso factum est nihil quod factum est. 4 In ipso vita erat, et vita erat lux hominum: 5 et lux in tenebris lucet, et tenebrae eam non comprehenderunt. 6 (2.3) Fuit homo missus a deo, cui nomen erat Iohannes: 7 hic venit in testimonium, ut testimonium perhiberet de lumine, ut omnes crederent per illum. 8 Non erat ille lux, sed ut testimonium perhiberet de lumine. 9 (3.3) Erat lux vera, quae inluminat omnem hominem venientem in mundum. 10 In mundo

Evangelium St. Johannis.

I.

Vom fleischgewordenen Worte Gottes. Johannis des Täufers Zeugnisse von Christo. Die ersten Jünger: Andreas, Johannes, Petrus, Philippus und Nathanael.

1 Im Anfang war das Wort, und das Wort war bey Gott, und Gott war das Wort. 2 Dasselbige war im Anfang bey Gott. 3 Alle Dinge sind durch dasselbige gemacht, und ohn dasselbige ist nichts gemacht was gemacht ist. 4 In ihm war das Leben, und das Leben war das Licht der Menschen. 5 Und das Licht scheinet in der Finsterniß, und die Finsterniß habens nicht begriffen. 6 Es ward ein Mensch von Gott gesandt, der hieß Johannes. 7 Derselbige kam zum Zeugniß, daß er von dem Licht zeugete, auf daß sie alle durch ihn glaubten. 8 Er war nicht das Licht, sondern daß er zeugete von dem Licht. 9 Das war das wahrhaftige Licht, welchs alle Menschen er-

▲ Constantine von Tischendorf published a "triglot" New Testament in 1854. It contained the Greek New Testament, the Latin, and the German.

▼ **A LEAF FROM THE LONDON POLYGLOT BIBLE PUBLISHED IN 1655** This leaf from Exodus contains an Aramaic Targum (Onkelos), the Samaritan Pentateuch, and an Arabic version—each with Latin translations. The facing page (not pictured) included the Hebrew text, Septuagint, and a Syriac version—each with Latin translations.

SAMUEL BAGSTER'S 1841 HEXAPLA OF THE NEW TESTAMENT

The heading of every page contained the Greek New Testament. Below it in parallel columns were the English versions of Wycliffe, Tyndale, Cranmer (the "Great Bible"), the Geneva Bible, the Rheims-Douay, and the King James Version.

▲ The fifth-century Codex Bezae, the oldest preserved bilingual manuscript, contained the Greek text on the left page and the Latin text on the right.

► **JOHN WESLEY (1703–1791)** preaching from the Scriptures in the old Cripplegate Church in London. Tens of thousands of people heard the biblical preaching of Wesley and his friend, George Whitefield.

◄ **J. HUDSON TAYLOR (1832–1905)** was an English missionary who spent the greater part of his life in China. He translated the Scriptures into a Chinese tongue and worked tirelessly, in spite of health problems and trials, to bring God's Word to the Chinese. He became the founder of China Inland Mission (now Overseas Missionary Fellowship).

TAKING THE BIBLE TO THE WORLD

Convinced that the Bible is the life-changing Word of God, many Christians have made enormous sacrifices and risked their lives to tell people the message of liberation from sin and reconciliation to God found in its pages. They were inspired by the original Apostles, who spread the good news of Jesus Christ throughout the Mediterranean world. Not a century has gone by without followers of Jesus taking their Bibles and sharing its content with people on the Continent, the British Isles, the Far East, and everywhere in between. Many, such as John Wycliffe, believed that the best way for people to hear and receive the Bible was to make it available in the language of the people. Missionaries often invested countless hours in learning new languages and translating the Bible. Hudson Taylor, for instance, spent five years translating the New Testament into the Ningpo dialect in China. Their efforts have resulted in countless numbers from every land on earth becoming Christians and experiencing God's blessing. The work continues.

◄ **DAVID LIVINGSTONE (1813–1873)** was a Scottish missionary, medical worker, and explorer in Africa in the mid–1800s. He took the gospel to parts of Africa where no explorer had ever been.

▲ **WILLIAM CAREY (1761–1834)** was an English missionary to India. He completed translations of the Bible into Bengali, Sanskrit, and Marathi in addition to organizing schools and preaching.

JOHN WYCLIFFE (1330–1384)

inspired a group of followers, known as "Lollards," who traveled throughout England proclaiming the gospel and calling people back to a more biblical Christianity. The Lollards believed that the Bible was the sole authority for faith and practice, and that every person had the right to read and interpret it.

▲ The youthful Billy Graham preaching from his Bible to a crowd of British people assembled at Trafalgar Square on April 3, 1954. Appeals to the Bible were always central to Graham's preaching.

◄ **BILLY GRAHAM** preaching from his Bible to 75,000 people in San Antonio, Texas.

TRANSLATING THE BIBLE FOR THE YALI PEOPLE OF INDONESIA

▲ A young Yali woman named Deratina reads the words of the Scripture in her native language.

Joyous feasting and celebration marked the dedication of the Yali Bible on May 16, 2000. This was the first complete Bible to be translated and published in any of the 240 languages of Papua, Indonesia. The Yali had not always been excited about the gospel. Men from the tribe shot and killed two missionaries in 1968. Two years earlier, their arrows felled two Yali believers when they tried to take the gospel to their own people. But visit a Yali village today and you will see men, women, and children reading the Scriptures, and packed church services with open Bibles on the laps of people eagerly following the message. The translation work was be-

gun by Stan Dale but was abruptly interrupted in 1968 when he was killed. Bruno de Leeuw resumed the task and was joined in 1974 by John and Gloria Wilson, who brought it to completion. Since no Yali could read and the language had no written form, John had to analyze it, develop a script, then devise a literacy course and teach people to read and write. John enlisted the help of two Yali nationals, Luliap Bahabol and Otto Kobak, to assist in the project. He instructed them in translation principles, and together they participated in translation workshops organized by the Indonesian Bible Society. With encouragement from Dr. Daud Soesilo, a United Bible Societies translation consultant, the Yali men accepted more and more responsibility and persevered through many difficulties until the whole Bible was translated.

◀ The arrival of the first published Yali Bibles.

▲ Otto works on the Yali translation with the help of John Wilson (right) and the United Bible Societies' consultant, Dr. Daud Soesilo.

▲ Psalm 23 in the Yali Bible.

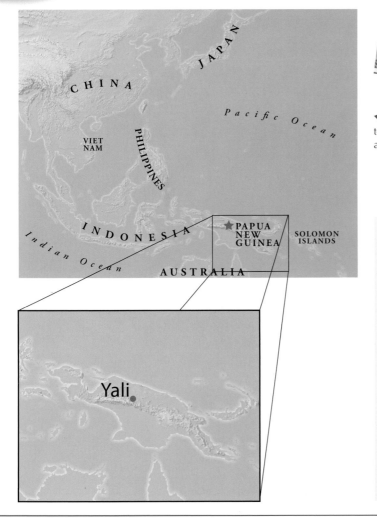

▲ A crowd of Yali people at the dedication of the Bible in 2000.

▼ Luliap and Otto learn to edit on the computer.

◀ Key members of the translation team: (l. to r.) Luliap, Bruno, Otto, and John.

CHINA

JAPAN

VIET NAM

PHILIPPINES

Pacific Ocean

INDONESIA

Indian Ocean

AUSTRALIA

★ PAPUA NEW GUINEA

SOLOMON ISLANDS

Yali

The United Bible Societies is the world fellowship of 137 National Bible Societies serving in over 200 countries and territories. The Societies join together for consultation, mutual support, and action in their task of translating. They endeavor to achieve the widest possible distribution of the Scriptures while also working to help people interact meaningfully with the Word of God. Bible Societies seek to carry out their task in partnership and cooperation with all Christian churches and church-related organizations.

▲ Suleiman Galadima quotes from the Cishingini translation of Luke to his blind father.

▶ Deacon Audu Auna spoke for people around the world when he held the Tsikimba translation of Genesis in his hand and said, "Now we know what God is saying to us."

TRANSLATING THE BIBLE FOR THE PEOPLE OF KAMBARI, AFRICA

▲ Saratu Ma'iwan reads to her daughter from the recently translated book of Genesis.

Three tribes in western Nigeria have never had Bibles in their own languages, but this is about to change. In 1988, the husband and wife team of John and Janie Stark traveled to the Kambari area of Nigeria (near Lake Kanji) to begin the long and arduous process of translating the Scriptures into the three distinct local languages. To turn the hope into reality, the Starks joined with interested individuals from each of the three language groups. Before they could begin, however, groundwork needed to be laid for this project. Never before had the three languages of the Kambari been put into written form. The translation team started by developing a writing system that would work well for each of the three languages. They also produced teaching materials and organized volunteer literacy teachers. The three translations are well underway. Portions of the Bible have already been translated, printed, and distributed in the three different languages of the area.

wovon.

⁶ Avu u damma le, "She i uwa asalama wan. N reve tạ i te e izami yạ Yesu za Nazara za na a varai a aakpata. Wu pa shi. A 'yasan yi tạ. Kalyuwai ubạtạ u na u danai. ⁷ 'Yawai i damma ojoro ạ yi nạ Bituru u tạ ɗe elime ạ ɗu ạ 'yawạ Galili. I te ene yi ununa u damma ndu."

⁸ Ana o utại, avu a suma ni iladi. Reve e reme asalama nạ meje'en mạ lipu. A damma za shi, adama a na wovon u reme nle.

Yesu 'yawạ tạ ubạtạ wạ Meri Magadaliya

⁹ [Nu usana u na Yesu 'yoyin o rana wa Aladi, Meri Magadaliya ɗa fara ene niyi, za na wu utại otoni ạ limạ e cindere atsumạ ạ yi. ¹⁰ U damma tạ aza a na ạ danai obolo nạ yi, a na ạ danai a sali nạ

---

atsumolạngu. ¹¹ Ana a uwwai u tu wuma, sapu we ene yi, reve a 'yuwan ạ usu.

Yesu roco tạ aciyạyi ubạta wo ojoro e re

¹² Ana addama o ndolo o kotoi, avu Yesu tạwạ ubạtạ wa ama e re oroci a vuma, ele ạ mmalu o ure ạ tyo ạ mạlyuci. ¹³ Avu ạ 'yawạ a damma akapi'i, agba ạ usu shi.

Wilạ u na Yesu cayi ojoro kupa nạ za tạ

¹⁴ Nạ ạcapạ a ɗa u tawại ubạtạ wo ojoro kupa nạ za tạ'ạ, ele nden a alya e ilyalya. Avu u yuwaan le nlạngi adama o okolo o ugbamu u le nu ulambu u na a cayi okolo shi. Adama a na a 'yuwain ạ usu ili i na aza a na e ene niyi a damma nle cina u 'yon. ¹⁵ Avu u damma le, "Yawai atsumạ o uvaɗi suru i yuwaan ama alajiya a alabari a sa'ani. ¹⁶ Za na usuyi ạ rumbu niyi waru, a ta wawa yi. Amma za na

◄ Mark 16 in Tsishingini, one of the three languages of the Kambari Language Project

---

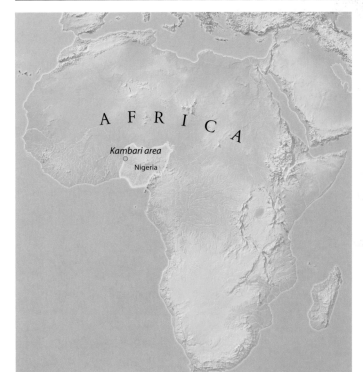

The organization behind this project, Wycliffe Bible Translators, is part of a global Bible translation movement working toward beginning translation in each of the remaining 3,000 Bible-less language communities by the year 2025. From its inception in 1934, Wycliffe Bible Translators has served over 1,800 people groups by helping to translate the Scriptures for those who have no Bible in their heart language.

◄ Cutting-edge technology serves as a digital helper in translation projects worldwide.

THE LIVING BIBLE

▲ Ken Taylor presented the first copy of the Living Bible to Billy Graham at a crusade in 1971. Dr. Graham heartily supported the Living Bible.

With a house full of children and a heart determined to help them know God's word, Ken Taylor was puzzled over what to do when his kids had difficulty understanding the King James Bible as he read it to them. Stopping every few minutes to explain what it said helped, but how much better it would be if they could be gripped by its words as they heard them. After praying and thinking over this issue, the thought came to him in 1955, "what about restating each verse to make it more understandable?" This was the catalyst for the creation of the Living Bible. Over the next few years, while riding a commuter train to work in Chicago, Ken began writing a paraphrase of the Bible in common everyday English. As the basis for his paraphrase, he used the American Standard Version of 1901. His first installment, the letters of Paul, was completed in 1962 and published under the title, Living Letters. In 1971, the entire Bible was published as The Living Bible. After a slow beginning, The Living Bible became extremely popular among English-speaking people throughout the world. It has sold over 40 million copies.

TEXT COMPARISON: ROMANS 3:24–25

KJV "Being justified freely by his grace through the redemption that is in Christ Jesus: Whom God hath set forth to be a propitiation through faith in his blood,"

LB "yet now God declares us 'not guilty' of offending him if we trust in Jesus Christ, who in his kindness freely takes away our sins. For God sent Christ Jesus to take the punishment for our sins and to end all God's anger against us. He used Christ's blood and our faith as the means of saving us from his wrath."

► A comparison of Romans 3:24–25 in the two versions.

◄ Tyndale House Publishers commissioned ninety scholars to produce a translation of the Bible based on the original languages but with the goal of approaching the readability of the Living Bible. The end result was published in 1996 and called the New Living Translation.

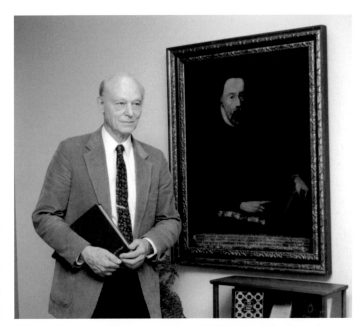

◄ Ken Taylor in his study, working on the Living Bible.

▲ Portrait of Ken Taylor and family in 1957.

▲ Ken Taylor pictured next to a portrait of William Tyndale, after whom Tyndale House Publishers was named.

◄ The Living Bible had a significant impact on the lives of many young people during the Jesus Movement in the late 1960s and early 1970s. This is a picture of Woodstock in 1969.

A COMPARISON OF MODERN VERSIONS OF THE BIBLE

More versions of the Bible are currently available in English than ever before in history. This is a great blessing and benefit, but many people wonder why there are so many translations and what the differences are between them. There are two important reasons for this proliferation of translations. First, because English usage changes so rapidly, there is a need to revise and update translations on a regular basis. Second, there are different translation philosophies that lead to different kinds of translations. These philosophies represent two different poles on a spectrum ranging from exactness (to the original form) to readability. The side emphasizing exactness is widely referred to as "formal equivalence." This is where a translator tries as closely as possible to follow the grammatical form of the original text. The scholar attempts a "word-for-word" translation in which the goal is to stay as close as possible to the form of the text in the original language. The other end of the spectrum emphasizes readability and is commonly called "dynamic equivalence" (or "functional equivalence"). This could be described as a more "thought-for-thought" translation of the text, with little concern placed on matching the grammatical structure of the

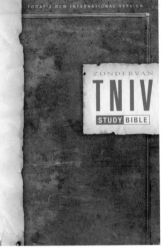

▲ Today's New International Version

original text. This approach endeavors to create a translation that can elicit an equivalence of response among contemporary readers similar to the way the Bible was heard and understood in its original setting. This approach strives to be as accurate as possible, too, but stresses accuracy of meaning over form.

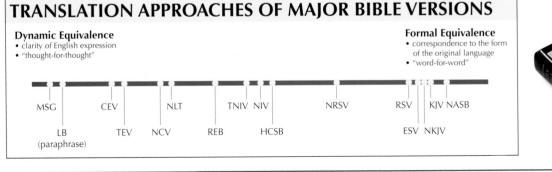

▲ The Message

▲ The New Living Translation

◀ The Contemporary English Version

▲ The English Standard Version

TRANSLATION APPROACHES OF MAJOR BIBLE VERSIONS

Dynamic Equivalence
• clarity of English expression
• "thought-for-thought"

Formal Equivalence
• correspondence to the form of the original language
• "word-for-word"

| MSG | | CEV | | NLT | | TNIV | NIV | | NRSV | | RSV | | KJV | NASB |

| | LB (paraphrase) | | TEV | | NCV | | REB | | HCSB | | | ESV | NKJV | |

CHARACTERISTICS OF MAJOR BIBLE VERSIONS

Version	Year Published	Characteristics	Grade Level	GN?	Apoc?
KJV King James Version	1611 1861* 1932* 1962*	• This is the most popular and widely used English Bible ever published. • The translators utilized a "literal" (formal equivalent) approach. • It has undergone three revisions and many changes since it was originally published in 1611. • The KJV is a revision of the Bishops' Bible (1568), which was a revision of the Great Bible (1539). • Sentence structure, expressions, and vocabulary represent Elizabethan-era English, making it difficult for many to understand today. • The KJV uses a different manuscript basis from other modern versions.	12.0		X
NKJV New King James Version	1979 NT 1982*	• The NKJV is an update and modernization of the KJV. • The original translators and updaters utilized a literal (formal equivalent) approach. • The translators replaced all the Elizabethan English with modern English. • The NKJV uses a different manuscript basis from other modern versions.	9.00		
RSV Revised Standard Version	1952 1971*	• This is a revision of the American Standard Version (1901), but less literal. • It became the most ecumenical version, accepted, and used by Protestant, Roman Catholic, and Eastern Orthodox believers.	NA		X
NRSV New Revised Standard Version	1990	• This is a revision of the RSV. • As the most ecumenical version, it is accepted and used by Protestant, Roman Catholic, and Eastern Orthodox believers.	10.4	X	X
ESV English Standard Version	2001	• The ESV is an evangelical revision of the RSV. • It is an "essentially literal" (formal equivalent) translation.	NA		
NASB New American Standard Bible	1971 1995*	• The NASB is one of the most literal (formal equivalent) translations available. • It was produced between 1959 and 1971 by 58 evangelical scholars from a variety of Bible denominations. • It is based on the American Standard Version (1901).	11.0		
NIV New International Version	1978	• The NIV is the most popular evangelical translation. • It attempts to find an optimal balance between exactness (formal equivalence) and readability (dynamic equivalence). • It was produced by a team of evangelical scholars, all of whom were committed "to the authority and infallibility of the Bible as God's Word In written form."	7.8		
TNIV Today's New International Version	2002	• This is an update and revision of the popular NIV. • The TNIV was translated by the Committee on Bible Translation, the same body of scholars that produced the NIV.	7.8	X	
HCSB Holman Christian Standard Bible	2000	• Like the NIV, this translation endeavors to maintain an optimum balance between exactness (formal equivalence) and readability (dynamic equivalence). • Commissioned by the Southern Baptist publishing house of Holman Bible Publishers, this translation was produced by a team of 90 scholars from a variety of denominations.	NA		
REB Revised English Bible	1989	• The REB is a revision of the New English Bible (1970). • It is a thought-for-thought (dynamic equivalent) translation produced in Great Britain. • The translation reflects many British idioms.	NA	X	X
TEV Today's English Version	1966 NT 1976	• This thought-for-thought (dynamic equivalent) translation was produced by the American Bible Society. • It makes use of colloquial English.	7.29		X
LB Living Bible	1967 NT 1971	• The LB is not a translation, but a paraphrase of the American Standard Version (1901) in understandable and colloquial English. • This Bible was produced by Kenneth N. Taylor, who decided to paraphrase the ASV to help his 10 children understand the Scriptures. • More than 40 million copies have been printed.	8.3		
NCV New Century Version	1991	• This dynamic translation was based on the International Childrens' Bible (1986). • It uses vocabulary at a third-grade level and avoids long sentences.	NA	X	
CEV Contemporary English Version	1995	• This dynamic modern-language translation was produced by the American Bible Society.	5.4	X	X
NLT New Living Translation	1996	• This is an actual translation—not a paraphrase—using a dynamic-equivalence approach. • The translation was completed by a team of 90 evangelical scholars from various denominations.	6.3	X	
The Message	1993 NT 2002	• The Message is an actual translation—not a paraphrase—into idiomatic English (the way we actually speak and think). • It often uses additional details to convey a thought.	4.8		

* = a second (or later) edition   NT = the New Testament portion   GN = **X** indicates that the translation is gender neutral.
Apoc = **X** indicates that the Apocrypha is available in this translation. Grade Level = This is an index for assessing the readability of the translation according to grade level. These figures are based on a study conducted by Swinburne Readability Laboratory (Charlottesvllle, Virginia). While the TNIV was not included in the study, the grade level remains the same as the NIV.

IS THE BIBLE STILL ACCURATE AFTER 2,000 YEARS?

A message can sometimes become garbled and distorted when it is passed on from one person to another a in a series. This can be illustrated in a simple classroom activity where the teacher tells a short story to one student and then instructs that student to tell another, and that one tells another, until it has passed through every student in the class. The end story is often so different that it is quite humorous. Is this what has happened to the Bible as it has been passed on over the past 2,000 years? The answer to this question is emphatically, no! The Bible has been transmitted through a very careful process with many checks and balances along the way. Furthermore, the scribes working on copying the text of Scripture took extraordinary care not to make careless mistakes. For instance, in one ancient Jewish document—the Babylonian Talmud—a Rabbinic scribe says, "My son, be careful, because your work is the work of heaven; should you omit even one letter or add even one letter, the whole world would be destroyed." This kind of utmost seriousness and care characterized the scribes who worked on the New Testament documents as well. Today we also possess the advantage having many ancient manuscripts that can be dated back not far from the originals. When we compare these to the Bibles we use today, the result is an astonishing degree of correspondence.

▲ **THE FAMOUS ISAIAH SCROLL FROM QUMRAN (1QIsᵃ)** In a comparison of a sample of thirteen verses (Isa 50:7–51:10) between the Qumran scroll and Codex Leningradensis, copied a thousand years later, the text was virtually identical. There were only four differences in minor details and two differences in orthography.

Tacitus—*Annals*
3 manuscripts

Plato—*Crito, Phaedo*
6 manuscripts

Thucydides—*History*
7 manuscripts

Julius Caesar—*Gallic War*
10 manuscripts

◀ **A SMALL PAPYRUS FRAGMENT** of the gospel of John found in Egypt and published in 1983. The fragment dates to the second century AD, making it one of the oldest copies of the New Testament that we have. This fragment was among the finds at Oxyrhynchus and has been designated 𝔓⁹⁰. It contains John 18:36–19:7 on both sides.

A Comparison Between the New Fragment and Our Greek New Testament
(John 18:36-19:7; 11 verses)
Where is it different than the United Bible Society's edition of the Greek text?

verse	Comparison with the new fragment (exactly the same unless otherwise noted)
18:36	
18:37	• two words in a different order
18:38	
18:39	• different spelling of one word • inserts a particle to indicate a purpose clause
18:40	
19:1	• different grammatical form of the same word • Pilate spelled differently (*peilatos*)
19:2	
19:3	
19:4	• difference in emphasis: "I find not one bit of guilt…" (UBS) versus "I find no guilt in him" (new)
19:5	
19:6	• different grammatical form of same word • difference in emphasis: "crucify, crucify" (UBS) versus "crucify him" (new) • different word order for two words
19:7	

Conclusions: (1) the degree of identity is extraordinary, and (2) not one of the differences affects the meaning of the text in any way.

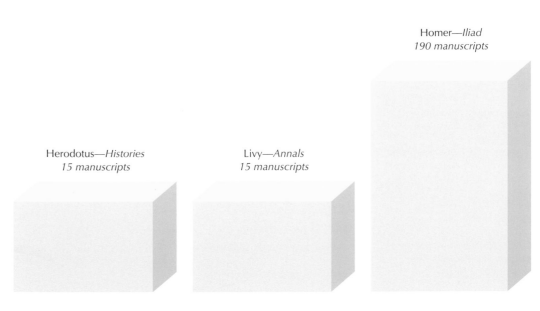

Herodotus—*Histories*
15 manuscripts

Livy—*Annals*
15 manuscripts

Homer—*Iliad*
190 manuscripts

PHOTO CREDITS

1–The Oldest Forms of the Bible Ever Discovered

Silver scroll	Z. Radovan/www.BibleLandPictures.com
Nash papyrus	Z. Radovan/www.BibleLandPictures.com
Psalms scroll	© Topham/The Image Works
Oldest fragment of New Testament	Reproduced by courtesy of the University Librarian and Director, The John Rylands University Library, The University of Manchester
Codex Sinaiticus	Photograph of 1911 facsimile edition
Codex Cairensis	Jewish National and University Library, Jerusalem, Israel

2–Alphabets, Animal Hides, and Papyrus

Papyrus reeds	John Feeney/Saudi Aramco World/PADIA
Creating papyrus paper	John Feeney/Saudi Aramco World/PADIA
Finished piece of papyrus	John Feeney/Saudi Aramco World/PADIA
Vellum	Z. Radovan/www.BibleLandPictures.com
Gilgamesh epic	Z. Radovan/www.BibleLandPictures.com
Ancient stylus and inkwell	Réunion des Musées Nationaux/Art Resource, NY
Scroll of Hebrew Bible	Réunion des Musées Nationaux/Art Resource, NY

3–The Principal Manuscript Behind the Old Testament

A leaf from the Aleppo Codex	Z. Radovan/www.BibleLandPictures.com
Drawing of Tiberius	Z. Radovan/www.BibleLandPictures.com
A leaf from Codex Lenigradensis	Photograph by Bruce and Kenneth Zuckerman, West Semitic Research with the collaboration of the Ancient Biblical Manuscript Center. Courtesy Russian National Museum (Saltyov-Shchedrin)
Illumination from Codex Lenigradensis	Photograph by Bruce and Kenneth Zuckerman, West Semitic Research with the collaboration of the Ancient Biblical Manuscript Center. Courtesy Russian National Museum (Saltyov-Shchedrin)
Portion of Masorah from Codex Lenigradensis	Photograph by Bruce and Kenneth Zuckerman, West Semitic Research with the collaboration of the Ancient Biblical Manuscript Center. Courtesy Russian National Museum (Saltyov-Shchedrin)
Genesis 1 in Hebrew Bible scholars use today	Clinton E. Arnold

4–The Hebrew Bible is Translated into Greek

Earliest surviving portions of Greek Bible	Reproduced by courtesy of the University Librarian and Director, The John Rylands University Library, The University of Manchester
Portion of Septuagint found at Qumran	Courtesy Israel Antiquities Authority
Leaf from Codex Sinaiticus	Photograph of 1911 facsimile edition
First page of Genesis from Septuagint by UBS	*Septuaginta*, edited by Alfred Rahlfs, 1935 and 1979 Deutsche Bibelgesellschaft, Stuttgart. Used by permission.
Illumination from Ruskin Septuagint	The Scriptorium: Center for Biblical Antiquities, Orlando, Florida
Form of Septuagint used by scholars today	*Septuaginta*, edited by Alfred Rahlfs, 1935 and 1979 Deutsche Bibelgesellschaft, Stuttgart. Used by permission.

5–The Hebrew Bible into Many Other Languages

Coptic (Egyptian) manuscript	The Scriptorium: Center for Biblical Antiquities, Orlando, Florida
Latin manuscript of Exodus	The Scriptorium: Center for Biblical Antiquities, Orlando, Florida
Syriac ms. 7th century Syriac psalter	The Scriptorium: Center for Biblical Antiquities, Orlando, Florida
Tower of Babel	Erich Lessing/Art Resource, NY
Fragments of Aramaic Targum	Courtesy Israel Antiquities Authority

6–The Dead Sea Scrolls

Aerial view of Qumran	Z. Radovan/www.BibleLandPictures.com
Isaiah Scroll	© John C. Trever, PhD, courtesy of the Trever family
Israeli Archaeologist Yigael Yadin	Z. Radovan/www.BibleLandPictures.com
Entrance of Cave 4	Clinton E. Arnold
Inkwell	Erich Lessing/Art Resource, NY
Pottery jar	© AAAC/Topham/The Image Works

7–What Is the Old Testament?

Torah Scroll	© Topham/The Image Works
Ur of the Chaldees	Tor Eigeland/Saudi Aramco World/PADIA
Temple of Solomon	© Hugh Claycombe
Chart of the books by kind	Clinton E. Arnold
Timeline of the OT writings	Clinton E. Arnold

8–The Apocrypha

Coin of Antiochus IV Epiphanes	Erich Lessing/Art Resource, NY
Judas Maccabeus	© Topham/The Image Works
Catholic Study Bible	Clinton E. Arnold
The end of the Book of Tobit from Codex Sinaiticus	Photograph of 1911 facsimile edition
Leaf of 1 Macc from KJV 1611 Apocrypha	Biola University Library Archives (photo by Clinton E. Arnold)
Martin Luther	© Topham/The Image Works

9–An Ancient Storeroom of Manuscripts: The Cairo Genizah

Eben Ezrah Synagogue	Z. Radovan/www.BibleLandPictures.com
Leather Torah scroll	Used with permission of the Syndics of the Cambridge University Library, Cambridge, England
Paper leaf from a codex	Used with permission of the Syndics of the Cambridge University Library, Cambridge, England
Verso side of Geniza fragment	Used with permission of the Syndics of the Cambridge University Library, Cambridge, England
Solomon Schechter	Used with permission of the Syndics of the Cambridge University Library, Cambridge, England
Codex Cairensis	Jewish National and University Library, Jerusalem, Israel

10–An Ancient Repository of Manuscripts in the Sinai Desert

St. Catherine's monastery	Z. Radovan/www.BibleLandPictures.com
Ceiling of manuscript storeroom	Daniel B. Wallace, Center for the Study of New Testament Manuscripts
Leaf from Codex Sinaiticus	Photograph of 1911 facsimile edition
Close-up of Codex Sinaiticus	Photograph of 1911 facsimile edition
Constantine von Tischendorf	Clinton E. Arnold
Greek New Testament	Clinton E. Arnold

11–Early Papyrus Texts of the New Testament

Late 2nd century fragment of Matthew 21	Egyptian Exploration Society, London, England
3rd century fragment of Hebrews 1:7–12	Egyptian Exploration Society, London, England
1903 excavations	Egyptian Exploration Society, London, England

A leaf from papyrus codex of Paul University of Michigan
Title page of an Oxyrhynchus Volume
　　　　Biola University Library Archives
　　　　(photo by Clinton E. Arnold)
Sample page from P.Oxy Volume Biola University Library Archives
　　　　(photo by Clinton E. Arnold)
Published Oxyrhynchus Biola University Library Archives
　　　　(photo by Clinton E. Arnold)
List of ancient papyri Clinton E. Arnold

12–Early Parchment Manuscripts of the Bible

Leaf from Codex Vaticanus (B) © Biblioteca Apostolica Vaticana (Vatican)
Leaf from Codex Bezae (D) Used with permission of the Syndics of the
　　　　Cambridge University Library, Cambridge,
　　　　England
Leaf from Codex Alexandrinus (A) By permission of the British Library
B.F. Westcott © Topham/The Image Works
Wescott-Hort Greek New Testament Biola University Library Archives
　　　　(photo by Clinton E. Arnold)
Chart of the uncial manuscripts Clinton E. Arnold

13–5,000 Greek Manuscripts from the Middle Ages

Chart of NT minuscule manuscripts Clinton E. Arnold
Sample variation between textural families
　　　　Clinton E. Arnold
Hagia Sophia Bildarchiv Preussischer Kulturbesitz/
　　　　Art Resource, NY
Minuscule manuscript of Acts The Scriptorium: Center for Biblical
　　　　Antiquities, Orlando, Florida
Codex manuscript from 9th century The Scriptorium: Center for Biblical
　　　　Antiquities, Orlando, Florida
Thirteenth century codex of gospels
　　　　Daniel B. Wallace, Center for the Study of
　　　　New Testament Manuscripts
Beginning of Mark's gospel Clinton E. Arnold

14–The Bible Is Translated into Latin

Leaf from 13th-century Latin Vulgate
　　　　The Scriptorium: Center for Biblical
　　　　Antiquities, Orlando, Florida
Page from Latin Vulgate of 1225 The Scriptorium: Center for Biblical
　　　　Antiquities, Orlando, Florida
Illumination of the scribe Ezra Scala/Art Resource, NY
Artistic rendition of Jerome Réunion des Musées Nationaux/
　　　　Art Resource, NY
Latin Vulgate from 1280 Biola University Library Archives
　　　　(photo by Clinton E. Arnold)
Close-up of Latin Vulgate from 1280 Biola University Library Archives
　　　　(photo by Clinton E. Arnold)

15–The Largest and Heaviest Manuscript of the Bible

Cover of Codex Gigas The Royal Library, National Library of Sweden
Page from Codex Gigas The Royal Library, National Library of Sweden
Illumination of the devil The Royal Library, National Library of Sweden
Close-up illumination from Codex Gigas
　　　　The Royal Library, National Library of Sweden
Miniature Bible Biola University Library Archives
　　　　(photo by Clinton E. Arnold)

16–The New Testament Is Translated into Other Languages

Ethiopic copy of the gospels The Scriptorium: Center for Biblical
　　　　Antiquities, Orlando, Florida
Copy of the gospels in Slavonic The Scriptorium: Center for Biblical
　　　　Antiquities, Orlando, Florida
Decorative cover to a 1659 copy of Armenian gospels
　　　　The Scriptorium: Center for Biblical
　　　　Antiquities, Orlando, Florida
Syriac manuscript The Scriptorium: Center for Biblical
　　　　Antiquities, Orlando, Florida
Close-up of illumination Biola University Library Archives
　　　　(photo by Clinton E. Arnold)
Illumination of Peter and Paul © The British Library/HIP/The Image Works
Map Clinton E. Arnold

17–What Is the New Testament?

Chart of the New Testament books by contents and date
　　　　Clinton E. Arnold
Two panel image of Christ's crucifixion and image of an animal slain on the altar
　　　　© Topham/The Image Works
11th-century Anglo-Saxon relief © The British Museum/HIP/The Image Works
Illumination of Pentecost © The British Library/HIP/The Image Works
List of books of the New Testament Biola University Library Archives
　　　　(photo by Clinton E. Arnold)
Illustration of Christ's victory over death
　　　　Biola University Library Archives
　　　　(photo by Clinton E. Arnold)

18–Illuminated Manuscripts

Codex Purpureus rossanensis Scala/Art Resource, NY
Illumination of Luke Werner Forman/Art Resource, NY
The symbol of Mark's gospel © Topham/The Image Works
Artistic representation of the name *Matthew*
　　　　Trinity College Library, Dublin, Ireland
Gospel symbols Trinity College Library, Dublin, Ireland
Representation of Jesus Trinity College Library, Dublin, Ireland

19–Scribes and Scriptoria

Illumination from a 15th-century manuscript
　　　　Z. Radovan/www.BibleLandPictures.com
Gregoriou Monastery © Topham/The Image Works
Iviron Monastery © Topham/The Image Works
Four crosses © Topham/The Image Works
Scribe at work © The British Library/HIP/The Image Works
Text of Eph 1:1 in Codex Sinaiticus Photograph of 1911 facsimile edition
Abbreviations of divine names Clinton E. Arnold
Scriptorium at Qumrun Clinton E. Arnold

20–The Earliest English Translations

Caedmon © Charles Walker/Topfoto/The Image Works
Oxfordshire clergyman © Charles Walker/Topfoto/The Image Works
Venerable Bede © Topham/The Image Works
Latin-English interlinear translation Art Resource, NY
Alfred the Great coin © The British Museum/HIP/The Image Works
Old English manuscript © Topham/The Image Works
Lindisfarne Castle © Topham/The Image Works
The Lindisfarne Gospels © The British Museum/HIP/The Image Works

21–The First Complete Bible in English: The Wycliffe Bible

John Wycliffe © The British Museum/HIP/The Image Works
Beginning of Mark's gospel © Lebrecht Music & Arts/The Image Works
Complete Wycliffe Bible The Scriptorium: Center for Biblical
　　　　Antiquities, Orlando, Florida
St. Paul's Cathedral Snark/Art Resource, NY
John Huss Foto Marburg/Art Resource, NY
Prologue to Matthew This item is reproduced by permission of the
　　　　Huntington Library, San Marino, California

22–The Invention of Printing: The Gutenberg Press

Gutenberg press Erich Lessing/Art Resource, NY
Beginning of Daniel from the Gutenberg Bible
　　　　The Scriptorium: Center for Biblical
　　　　Antiquities, Orlando, Florida
Page of Gutenberg Bible with illuminations
　　　　© 2002 ARPL/Topham/The Image Works
Mainz Cathedral © Axel Mosler/VISUM/The Image Works
Johannes Gutenberg Bildarchiv Preussischer Kulterbesitz/
　　　　Art Resource, NY
Entire Gutenberg Bible The Pierpont Morgan Library/
　　　　Art Resource,NY
Printed indulgence By permission of the British Library

23–The First Published Greek New Testament

Desiderius Erasmus Erich Lessing/Art Resource, NY
Title page of Erasmus's Greek New Testament
　　　　The Scriptorium: Center for Biblical
　　　　Antiquities, Orlando, Florida

12th century minuscule codex	Öffentliche Bibliothek, Universität Basel, Switzerland
Text of Acts 1	The Scriptorium: Center for Biblical Antiquities, Orlando, Florida
Romans 1 in Erasmus's Greek New Testament	Biola University Library Archives (photo by Clinton E. Arnold)
Chart: History of Greek Bible	Clinton E. Arnold
Text of 1 John 5:7–8 in Erasmus's Greek New Testament	This item is reproduced by permission of the Huntington Library, San Marino, California

24–William Tyndale (1494–1536) and the Tyndale Bible

Portrait of William Tyndale	© The British Museum/HIP/The Image Works
Tower at Magdalen College	© Woodmansterne/Topham/The Image Works
Romans 1 in 1534 edition	The Scriptorium: Center for Biblical Antiquities, Orlando, Florida
Illustration of altar	The Scriptorium: Center for Biblical Antiquities, Orlando, Florida
Illustration of priestly ephod on Aaron	The Scriptorium: Center for Biblical Antiquities, Orlando, Florida
Martyrdom and burning of Tyndale	From *The Acts and Monuments of John Foxe,* London: The Religious Tract Society, 1877

25–Martin Luther Translates the Bible for the German People

Portrait of Martin Luther	Erich Lessing/Art Resource, NY
Title page to a 1534 Luther Bible	The Scriptorium: Center for Biblical Antiquities, Orlando, Florida
1534 Luther Bible	The Scriptorium: Center for Biblical Antiquities, Orlando, Florida
Luther working on his translation	© Mary Evans Picture Library/The Image Works
Parish church at Wittenberg	© Topham/The Image Works
Contemporary Luther bible	*Die Bibel* nach der Übersetzung Martin Luther in der revidierten Fassung von 1984, durchgesehene Ausgabe in neuer Rechtschreibung, 1999 Deutsche Bibelgesellschaft, Stuttgart. Used by permission.
Luther's zeal	From Merle d'Aubigné, *History of the Great Reformation in Europe.* Philadelphia: William Flint & Co., 1870
Text of Isaiah 53 from Luther Bible	Biola University Library Archives (photo by Clinton E. Arnold)

26–Bible Translation During the Reign of Henry VIII

Portrait of Henry VIII	© Topham/The Image Works
Portrait of Sir Thomas Cromwell	© Print Collector/HIP/The Image Works
Mile Coverdale	© Topham/The Image Works
Title page of Coverdale Bible	The Scriptorium: Center for Biblical Antiquities, Orlando, Florida
Matthew's Bible opened to the gospel of John	Biola University Library Archives (photo by Clinton E. Arnold)
Title page of the Great Bible	© The British Library/HIP/The Image Works

27–John Calvin and the Geneva Bible (1560)

Portrait of John Calvin	Giraudon/Art Resource, NY
Queen Elizabeth I	© Woodmansterne/Topham/The Image Works
Introductory page of 1560 Geneva Bible	The Scriptorium: Center for Biblical Antiquities, Orlando, Florida
1583 edition of Geneva Bible	The Scriptorium: Center for Biblical Antiquities, Orlando, Florida

Table of contents from 1609 edition	Biola University Library Archives (photo by Clinton E. Arnold)
Gospel of John in 1609 edition	Biola University Library Archives (photo by Clinton E. Arnold)
Title page to 1609 edition	Biola University Library Archives (photo by Clinton E. Arnold)

28–Study Bibles

Geneva Bible	Biola University Library Archives (photo by Clinton E. Arnold)
Great Bible	Biola University Library Archives (photo by Clinton E. Arnold)
Luther Bible	Biola University Library Archives (photo by Clinton E. Arnold)
Matthew's Bible	Biola University Library Archives (photo by Clinton E. Arnold)
Map of Israel in the Bishop's Bible	Biola University Library Archives (photo by Clinton E. Arnold)
Coverdale Bible	The Scriptorium: Center for Biblical Antiquities, Orlando, Florida
Matthew's Bible notes	Biola University Library Archives (photo by Clinton E. Arnold)

29–The Predecessor to the King James Version: The Bishops' Bible (1568)

Matthew Parker	© Topham/The Image Works
Bishop's Bible 1568–introduction to the second part of the Bible	The Scriptorium: Center for Biblical Antiquities, Orlando, Florida
Genesis 1 with an illustration of the garden	The Scriptorium: Center for Biblical Antiquities, Orlando, Florida
Title page to the New Testament	Biola University Library Archives (photo by Clinton E. Arnold)
Isaiah 53:1–3 in 1575 edition	Biola University Library Archives (photo by Clinton E. Arnold)
Table on genealogies of Matthew and Luke	Biola University Library Archives (photo by Clinton E. Arnold)
Predecessors to the KJV chart	Clinton E. Arnold
Douay-Rheims Bible title page	The Scriptorium: Center for Biblical Antiquities, Orlando, Florida
Mark 1 in Douay-Rheims	The Scriptorium: Center for Biblical Antiquities, Orlando, Florida

30–The King James Version of 1611

James I of England and VI of Scotland	Erich Lessing/Art Resource, NY
Title page of King James Bible of 1611	The Scriptorium: Center for Biblical Antiquities, Orlando, Florida
Illustration of the family tree of Adam and Eve	The Scriptorium: Center for Biblical Antiquities, Orlando, Florida
Text of the ten commandments	The Scriptorium: Center for Biblical Antiquities, Orlando, Florida
Comma Johanneum	Biola University Library Archives (photo by Clinton E. Arnold)
King James with the Apocrypha	Biola University Library Archives (photo by Clinton E. Arnold)
Chart of some archaic expressions	Clinton E. Arnold

31–A Forbidden Book Worth Dying For

Queen Mary I	© Topham/The Image Works
Roman Emperor Diocletian	Erich Lessing/Art Resource, NY
Tyndale's bible being smuggled into England	© ARPL/HIP/The Image Works
Brother Andrew	Courtesy of Open Doors
Bible burning	Bruce M. Metzger
Exhumation of Wycliff	From *The Acts and Monuments of John Foxe,* London: The Religious Tract Society, 1877.

| Cuthbert Tunstall | From Merle d'Aubigné, *History of the Great Reformation in Europe.* |

32–The First Bible Printed in America: The Algonquin Bible (1663)

Title page of the Algonquin Bible 1663	The Scriptorium: Center for Biblical Antiquities, Orlando, Florida
Opened Algonquin Bible	The Scriptorium: Center for Biblical Antiquities, Orlando, Florida
Landing of Governor John Winthrop	The New York Public Library/ Art Resource, NY
John Eliot	This item is reproduced by permission of the Huntington Library, San Marino, California
Seal of the Massachusetts Bay Colony	Biola University Library Archives (photo by Clinton E. Arnold)
16th-century painting of an Algonquin Indian	© The British Museum/HIP/ The Image Works

33–A Monumental Revision of the King James Version

J. B. Lightfoot	© The British Museum/HIP/ The Image Works
Philip Schaff	© Topham/The Image Works
Statement of the translation principles	From C. J. Ellicott, Editor, et al., *The New Testament of our Lord and Saviour Jesus Christ, Translated out of the Greek: Being the Version Set Forth A.D. 1611, Compared with the Most Ancient Authorities and Revised, A.D. 1881.* Oxford: Oxford University Press, 1881.
Footnote on longer ending of Mark	From C. J. Ellicott, Editor, et al., *The New Testament of our Lord and Saviour Jesus Christ, Translated out of the Greek: Being the Version Set Forth A.D. 1611, Compared with the Most Ancient Authorities and Revised, A.D. 1881.* Oxford: Oxford University Press, 1881.
1869 edition of Tischendorfs Greek New Testament	Clinton E. Arnold
American Standard Version of 1901	From Philip Schaff, Editor, et al., *The Holy Bible, Containing the Old and New Testaments, Translated out of the Original Tongues, Being the Version Set Forth A.D. 1611, Compared with the Most Ancient Authorities and Revised A.D. 1881-1885, Newly Edited by the American Revision Committee A.D. 1901, Standard Edition.* New York: Thomas Nelson & Sons, 1901.
ASV text of Isaiah 52-53	From Philip Schaff, Editor, et al., *The Holy Bible, Containing the Old and New Testaments, Translated out of the Original Tongues, Being the Version Set Forth A.D. 1611, Compared with the Most Ancient Authorities and Revised A.D. 1881-1885, Newly Edited by the American Revision Committee A.D. 1901, Standard Edition.* New York: Thomas Nelson & Sons, 1901.
Wescott-Hort Greek New Testament	From Brook Foss Westcott and Fenton John Anthony Hort, Editors, *The New Testament in the Original Greek.* London: Macmillan, 1881.

34–Successors to the ASV: The Modern Versions

Chart of Successors to the ASF	Clinton E. Arnold
ASV 1901	Clinton E. Arnold
Bruce Metzger	Bruce M. Metzger
NRSV 1990	Clinton E. Arnold
NASB 1971	Clinton E. Arnold
NIV 1978	Clinton E. Arnold
TNIV 2005	Clinton E. Arnold

35–All Ancient Manuscripts in One Volume

| Committee members | Bruce M. Metzger |

Bible Hebraica Stuttgartensia: opened to Isaiah	*Septuaginta,* edited by Alfred Rahifs, 1935 and 1979 Deutsche Bibelgesellschaft, Stuttgart, Used by permission.
Footnote from the BHS Isaiah 53	Clinton E. Arnold
Greek New Testament opened to Ephesians 1	Clinton E. Arnold
Chart of what the notes indicate	Clinton E. Arnold
Biblia Hebraica Stuttgartensia	Clinton E. Arnold
Greek New Testament	*The Greek New Testament,* Fourth Revised Edition, edited by Barbara Aland, Kurt Aland, Johannes Karavidopoulos, Carlo M. Martini, and Bruce M. Metzger in cooperation with the Institute for New Testament Textual Research, Munster/Westphalia, 1993 Deutsche Bibelgesellschaft, Stuttgart. Used by permission.
Greek New Testament, Septuagint	*Septuaginta,* edited by Alfred Rahlfs, 1935 and 1979 Duetsche Bibelgesellschaft, Stuttgart. Used by permission.

36–Early Parallel Bibles

5th-century Codex Bezae	Used with the permission of the Syndics of the Cambridge University Library, Cambridge, England
Complutensian Polyglot	The Scriptorium: Center for Biblical Antiquities, Orlando, Florida
Leaf from London Polyglot Bible	Biola University Library Archives (photo by Clinton E. Arnold)
Hamburg Polyglot	Biola University Library Archives (photo by Clinton E. Arnold)
Tischendorf's Triglot New Testament	Clinton E. Arnold
Bagster's 1841 Hexapla	Biola University Library Archives (photo by Clinton E. Arnold)
Title page of Complutensian Polyglot	The Scriptorium: Center for Biblical Antiquities, Orlando, Florida

37–Taking the Bible to the World

John Wycliffe	© English Heritage/HIP/The Image Works
Billy Graham preaching to crowd in Trafalgar Square	© Topham/The Image Works
John Wesley	© Fotomas/Topham/The Image Works
Billy Graham	© Jack Kurtz/The Image Works
David Livingstone	From Horace Walter, *The Last Journals of David Livingstone in Central Africa.* Hartford, Conn.: R.W. Bliss & Co., 1875
William Carey	From Joseph Belcher, *William Carey: A Biography.* Philadelphia: American Baptist Publication, 1853
Hudson Taylor	From Marshall Broomhall, *Hudson Taylor. The Man Who Believed God.* London: China Inland Mission, 1930

38–Translating the Bible for the Yali People of Indonesia

Psalm 23 in Yali Bible	John and Gloria Wilson, World Team
Crowd of Yali people	John and Gloria Wilson, World Team
A young Yali woman named Deratina	John and Gloria Wilson, World Team
Otto works on the Tali translation	John and Gloria Wilson, World Team
Luliap and Otto learn to edit on the computer	John and Gloria Wilson, World Team
The arrival of the first published Yali Bibles	John and Gloria Wilson, World Team
Key members of the translation team	John and Gloria Wilson, World Team

39–Translating the Bible for the People of Kambari, Africa

Mark 16 in Tsishingini	John and Janie Stark, Wycliffe Bible Translators
Cutting edge technology	John and Janie Stark, Wycliffe Bible Translators
Alphabet chart for the Kambari language	John and Janie Stark, Wycliffe Bible Translators

Suleiman Galadima quotes from the Cishingini translation

        John and Janie Stark, Wycliffe Bible Translators

Saratu Ma'iwan reads to her daughter

        John and Janie Stark, Wycliffe Bible Translators

Deacon Audu Auna   John and Janie Stark, Wycliffe Bible Translators

40–The Living Bible

Ken Taylor and family	Tyndale House Publishers, Inc.
Ken Taylor in his study	Tyndale House Publishers, Inc.
Ken Taylor with Billy Graham	Tyndale House Publishers, Inc.
Ken Taylor by portrait of William Tyndale	
	Tyndale House Publishers, Inc.
Photo of "Reach Out"	Tyndale House Publishers, Inc.
Photo of 1971 Living Bible	Tyndale House Publishers, Inc.
Photo of the "Living Letters"	Tyndale House Publishers, Inc.
New Living Translation Bible	Tyndale House Publishers, Inc.
Woodstock 1969	© John Dominis/The Image Works
Text comparison chart	Clinton E. Arnold

41–A Comparison of Modern Versions of the Bible

Chart: translation approaches of major Bible versions

        Clinton E. Arnold

Chart: characteristics of major Bible versions

        Clinton E. Arnold

ESV	Clinton E. Arnold
CEV	Clinton E. Arnold
TNIV	Clinton E. Arnold
The Message	Clinton E. Arnold
NLT	Tyndale House Publishers, Inc.

42–Is the Bible Still Accurate After 2,000 Years?

Small papyrus fragment   Egyptian Exploration Society,
London, England

Chart: comparison beteween new fragment and Greek New Testament

        Clinton E. Arnold

Chart: comparing the number of extant manuscripts or other ancient works to
the New Testament   Clinton E. Arnold

Famous Isaiah scroll   Z. Radovan/www.BibleLandPictures.com

We want to hear from you. Please send your comments about this book to us in care of zreview@zondervan.com. Thank you.

ZONDERVAN.com/
AUTHORTRACKER
follow your favorite authors